www.mathgoo
— good

That's maths sorted

MATHS? DON'T PANIC

Volume 2 – Algebra, and Geometry

A Tutorial Course in Mathematics
For Years 7, 8, and 9 (Pupils aged 11 to 14)

By Alison Joiner BSc, MSc, MInstP, FRAS, FIAP

Alison Joiner has been tutoring students of all ages who find mathematics difficult to understand. She now offers you the explanations, tips and memory aids which have helped her other pupils and their parents!

First published 2016
Minor amendments May 2018

Copyright © M. Alison Joiner 2016

All rights reserved

No part of this publication may be reproduced, stored in a retrieval system, or transmitted in any form or by any means without the prior permission in writing of the publishers, nor be otherwise circulated in any form of binding or cover other than in that it which it is published and without a similar condition being imposed on the subsequent purchaser.

ISBN – 13 978-151-77 88 056
ISBN – 10   151-77 88 056

Acknowledgments

The Author would like to thank Zoë Ann Pollard for typing this book preparing all the diagrams and for numerous helpful suggestions.

She would also like to thank Tim Joiner for giving a great deal of help with the layout.

She would also like to thank the following friends and pupils for proof reading, error spotting, general advice and trials of this material

Waseem Ahamed	Shania Lockwood
Qassim Ahamed	Katy Joiner and Staff of
Sophia Boggis-Rolffe	Quentin House School
Cian Ball	Sam Lewis
Erin Baxter	Joshua P Pollard
Megan Greenfield	Emilia Parr
Margaret Greaves	Serena Sale
Charlies Harding	Evie Sale
Rebecca Harding	Rona Shaw
Tim Joiner	Izzie Swain
Lizie Ginns	Felicity White
Abigail Kenny	
Jack Leming	

Specification

The contents of this volume include the material required by the Department of Education's Specification for Key Stage 3 Mathematics dated September 2013.

The Author

With twenty years of teaching experience, Alison Joiner provides individual lessons for pupils of all ages, from remedial reading to undergraduate physics. She has used this wealth of experience to write books on "how to do maths", using the methods and explanations which make sense to her pupils.

She has been Head of Physics at a girl's public school, and Head of science at a comprehensive school. She has taught day release apprentices, and undergraduate physics. She has taught at a college of technology and in a sixth form college. In industry she carried out research on semi-conductors, radar and underwater acoustics. She was at one time Head of Mathematical Modelling for an international defense company.

She has a BSc, an MSc, and a Post Graduate Certificate in Education. She is a Member of the Institute of Physics, A Fellow of the Royal Astronomical Society, and a Fellow of the Institute of Analysts and Programmers.

"My pupils appreciate that I am always careful to explain the logical connections between mathematical and scientific topics. The tips and memory aids I use in this book have helped lots of other people. Many of my ex-pupils have gained good University Places some at Oxford and Cambridge"

Chapter	Contents	Page
	ALGEBRA	
	Introduction	1
1	What is Algebra?	3
2	Word Equations – Numbers and Letters in Equations	7
3	Powers	11
4	Roots	15
5	Powers and Reciprocals	19
6	Linear Equations	23
7	Brackets	27
8	Graphs. Plotting Points	31
9	Plotting Graphs	33
10	Straight Line Graphs	37
11	Lines with Negative Slopes	41
12	Horizontal Lines, Vertical Lines and Quadrants	43
13	Sequences or Series	45
14	Finding a Term in an Arithmetic Series	47
15	Arithmetic Series with Negative Differences	51
16	Arithmetic Series. Finding the nth Term	55
17	Geometric Series	59
18	Fibonacci and Other Series	63
19	Rearranging and Solving Equations	67
20	Simultaneous Equations, Introduction	75
21	Simultaneous Equations with the Same Sign	77
22	Simultaneous Equations with Different Constants	79
23	Graphs of Quadratic Equations	85
24	Factors. What are they?	101
25	Multiplying Factors	103
26	Factors. Multiplying Brackets	105
27	Using Linear Graphs to Solve Problems	111
28	Using Quadratic Graphs to Solve Problems	113
29	Exponential Graphs	123
30	Using Reciprocal graphs	127

Chapter	Contents	Page
	GEOMETRY (Sometimes known as Shapes)	
31	Geometry. Lines and Angles	129
32	Drawing Tools	133
33	Planes, Parallel Lines and Right Angles	135
34	Triangles	141
35	Similar Triangles and Maps	149
36	Quadrilaterals	155
37	Areas	159
38	Areas of Triangles	163
39	Perimeters and Areas of Rectangles	167
40	Right Angle Triangles - Pythagoras	173
41	Areas and perimeters of circles	177
42	Areas and Perimeters of Shapes	183
43	Pentagons, Hexagons Octagons	187
44	Volumes of Cubes, Cuboids	189
45	Prisms, Pyramids and Cylinders	193
46	Regular Solids	199
47	Spheres and Cones	201
48	Things to Remember	205
49	How to Pass Examinations	207
	Index	209

Exercises

Exercises	ALGEBRA	Page
1	What is Algebra?	5
2	Word Equations – Using Numbers in Equations	9
3	Powers	13
4	Roots	17
5	Powers and Reciprocals	21
6	Linear Equations	25
7	Brackets	29
8	There is no Exercise on this Chapter	
9	Plotting Graphs	35
10	Straight Line Graphs	39
11	There is no Exercise on this Chapter	
12	There is no Exercise on this Chapter,	
13	There is no Exercise on this Chapter	
14	Finding a Term in an Arithmetic Series	49
15	Arithmetic Series with Negative Differences	53
16	Finding the nth term in a series	57
17	Geometric Series	61
18	Fibonacci and Other Series	65
19	Rearranging and Solving Equations	73
20 - 22	Simultaneous Equations	83
23	Graphs of Quadratic Functions	93
24	Factors - What are they?	101
25	Multiplying Factors	103
26	Factors Multiplying Brackets	109
27	There is no Exercise on this Chapter,	
28	Using Quadratic Graphs to Solve Problems	116
29	There is no Exercise on this Chapter,	
30	There is no Exercise on this Chapter,	

Exercises

Exercises	GEOMETRY	Page
31-3	Geometry. Lines and Angles	139
34	Triangles	147
35	Similar Triangles and Maps	153
36	There is no Exercise on this Chapter	
37	Areas	161
38	Areas of Triangles	165
39	Perimeters and Areas of Rectangles	171
40	Right Angle Triangles - Pythagoras	175
41	Areas and Perimeters of Circles	181
42	Areas and Perimeters of Shapes	185
43	There is no Exercise on this Chapter	
44	Volumes of Cubes, Cuboids,	191
45	Prisms, Pyramids and Cylinders	197
46	There is no Exercise on this Chapter	
47	Regular Solids	203

Introduction

Volume 1 of **Maths? Don't Panic!** showed you the easiest way of doing arithmetic. It covered Adding, subtracting, multiplying and dividing. It showed you how to use fractions decimals and percentages; how to find square and cube roots.

Now we come to **algebra**. Mathematicians often find themselves having to do the same calculation over-and-over again, each time with slightly different sets of numbers. You might be asked to calculate the position of planets against the night sky for every day in the year. To make sure that a bridge is strong enough, you might be asked to work out the loads on the bridge when it is carrying different combinations of vehicles and people. It is easier to do this sort of calculation if you substitute letters for numbers, do the calculations once, and only put in a set of numbers right at the end. This is algebra. Using algebra saves time and effort. It is the easiest way of doing complex calculations.

Geometry was invented to help people lay out the boundaries between fields, and to plan buildings.

In land which regularly floods, the boundary marks can often be washed away. It is not much use saying "I own all the land between the river and those two trees" if the river has changed its course and the trees have disappeared. That way leads to arguments and fights. It is better to make careful measurements before the floods come. Then it is easier so work out where the boundaries ought to be.

Geometry (the word means Earth measurement) is an intensely practical subject. It is used by builders, surveyors, designers and architects, engineers and ship builders. It comes into the drawing of maps and the laying out of the steel plate which is to be welded together to build a ship. It is used by garden designers.

Knowledge of geometry will help you to buy the right amount of wall paper. It will save you money by telling you the right number of tiles you need to buy to tile a wall, and how many paving slabs you will need for a patio.

Key Stage 3 Maths Explained Volume 2 Algebra

This book will save you from panicking when you find you have to order a lot of expensive tiles. It shows you how, with a tape measures and pegs, you can lay out a garden feature which is at right angles to you house (not slightly crooked.)

Algebra will save you effort every time you are asked to work out anything which need the same basic calculation to be repeated a great many times.

This book ends, like the last one, with a short list of things it is worth remembering, and advice on how to pass examinations.

Don't panic! Use this book to help you understand how to do maths. Then it will seem easy.

Chapter 1 – What is Algebra?

Sometimes you have to do a lot of similar calculations. The method is the same; the numbers are different.

For example, when you are buying cakes for a group of friends you will say: "If one cake costs 30p, and there are six of us here, then the cost of six cakes will be 6 × 30 = 180p.

You have said: Cost = number of cakes × price of one cake.

Then this could be written as:
Price of one cake = **p**, number of cakes = **n**, and cost of all the cakes = **c**. You could then write c = n × p. This is algebra. You have put letters to stand for the cost of the cakes, the number of cakes and the price of one cake.

You wrote c = n × p which is **an algebraic equation**. You have used letters to stand for the words so that you can make a calculation more easily. You have used algebra. Algebra uses letters to stand for the numbers. You can then use those letters to say how the calculation must be done. You have written the equation as c = n × p. So, if you are buying six cakes and they are priced at 9p each, the total cost is now given by:

$$c = n \times p = 6 \times 9 = 54p.$$

Algebra shows you how to do calculations; it gives you the pattern. The pattern uses letters to tell you how to solve the problem. The pattern is called the **formula**. So, going back to the cakes, the formula giving the cost of cakes is:

$$c = n \times p \quad \text{---------------} \quad (1)$$

You have written the answers to a large number of questions. They give you an exact method for finding the answer to a particular question.

Key Stage 3 Maths Explained Volume 2 Algebra

Let's go back to the cakes.

You see cakes in a shop window. The price tag says 35p each. You have six friends coming round after school. As you will also want a cake for yourself, you will need to buy seven cakes.

Equation ① gives you the formula for finding the cost (c) of any number of cakes (n) at any price (p pence). So, the total cost for 7 cakes at 35p each will be:
c = n × p = 7 × 35 = £2·45.

If you are given the numbers for all but one of the letters you have to "find the missing number". In algebra the missing number is usually called y, and the one you are given is called x.

Here the way of writing the letters is x and y so that x is not confused with the multiply sign ×.

An example is: If $y = 4x$, then find y if $x = 2$.
Your answer would be –

$y = 4x$ (= 4 × x)
$x = 2$
$y = 4 × 2$
So $y = 8$

Here is another example. If $y = 3x$. What is the value of y if $x = 4$?
Your answer would be:

$y = 3x$
so $y = 3 × x$
as $x = 4$ $y = 3 × 4$
so $y = 12$

Chapter 1 – What is Algebra?

Yet another example: If $y = 4x$. What is the value of y if $x = 5$?

$$y = 4x$$
so $\quad y = 4 \times x$
as $x = 5 \quad y = 4 \times 5$
so $\quad y = 20$

A third example: If $y = 5x$. What is the value of y if $x = 5$?

$$y = 5x$$
so $\quad y = 5 \times x$
as $x = 5 \quad y = 5 \times 5$
so $\quad y = 25$

Exercise 1

Now try these calculations for yourself, with the working out exactly as in the example. This way you will understand and learn the method. Then the maths gets easier!

1) $y = 2x$ find y if   i) $x = 4$ ii) $x = 9$ iii) $x = 1$ iv) $x = 11$

2) $y = 3x$ find y if   i) $x = 2$ ii) $x = 5$ iii) $x = 4$ liv) $x = 9$

The answers are on the next page.

5

Key Stage 3 Maths Explained Volume 2 Algebra

Answers to Exercise 1

1)   i) $y = 8$ ii) $y = 18$ iii) $y = 2$ iv) $y = 22$

2)   i) $y = 6$ ii) $y = 15$ iii) $y = 12$ iv) $y = 27$

Chapter 2 – Word Equations

Word Equations.

Again, I am going to use shopping to explain what I mean by **word equations.** (In this chapter whenever I am referring to money I shall write the word pence in full.) After all, you understand shopping, so you can understand these bits of algebra.

If you go into a shop and buy some sweets costing 85 pence and you only have a £1 coin then you expect some change, 15 pence in this case.

Change = £1·00 minus 85 pence = the money you hand over minus the cost of the sweets.

So, your change   = 100 pence   minus 85 pence
                  = 15 pence

Or you could say;
        Change = money given, minus the cost of the sweets.

As in Chapter 1 the number you are finding is called y, the number you are given is called x. If there is a third letter it is called z or any other letter that hasn't already been used. So here the change you get is called y, the money you hand to the shop keeper is x and the cost of the sweets could be s. That means that if y is the change you get then, y = money given − cost. In the example at the start of the Chapter the 'change' is called y, the £1 is x and the 85p is s

So $y = x - s$
From the question x = £1 = 100 pence and s = 85 pence.
So y = 100 − 85 = 15

You MUST get the x and s into the SAME UNITS BEFORE putting the numbers into the equation.

Key Stage 3 Maths Explained - Volume 2 Algebra

So $y = x - 85$, or change = money paid − 85p (the price of the sweets)

y = 100 pence − 85 pence   (you paid with a £1 coin = 100p)
y = 15 pence

Answer y = 15 pence   So your change is 15 pence.

When you get x and s into the same units then you will get y in the same units as x and s. If x and s are in different units then you won't have the slightest idea of the units of y. Say for example y = £10 − 50p. If you are shopping then you will automatically change pounds to pence or (if you have enough) pence to pounds, so the equation becomes 100 pence − 50 pence. You must do the same thing for all values, convert a mixture of units to one unit. Then it is easy to add, subtract, multiply and divide, and know what units you end up with! If you get the units wrong you will get the wrong answer.

Remember both sides of all equations must be in the same units

Here is another example. You buy some cakes, say 6 of them.
Each cake costs x pence.
The cost of 6 cakes at x pence each is: $6 \times x$ pence = $6x$ pence.
You give the shopkeeper a £1 coin. What change do you get?
Call the change y.

Change = £1 minus $6x$ pence
Or more simply y = 100 pence minus $6x$ pence
                      = 100 - $6x$ pence

If the cost of 1 cake is 15 pence then x = 15 pence, so 6 cakes cost $6 \times 15 = 90$ pence.

y = 100 pence minus 90 pence
So y = 10 pence (which is your change)

Chapter 2 – Word Equations

Equations often come without stories, but that doesn't matter. If you have the question "$y = 4x + 6$ find y when $x = 9$" then simply write out the equation.

$$y = 4x + 6$$
which means $y = 4 \times x + 6$
put 9 for x $y = 4 \times 9 + 6$
work it out $y = 36 + 6$
$$y = 42$$

Remember Multiply before you add

Exercise 2

1) $y = 3x + 2$ find y if $x = 4$

2) $y = 5x + 6$ find y if $x = 7$

3) $y = 2x - 7$ find y if $x = 9$

4) $y = 6x - 3$ find y if $x = 5$

5) $y = 7x + 4$ find y if $x = 8$

6) $y = 4x - 7$ find y if $x = 6$

7) $y = 3x + 4$ find y if $x = 3$

8) $y = 3x - 6$ find y if $x = 10$

9) $y = 5x + 3$ find y if $x = 7$

10) $y = 11x - 10$ find y if $x = 4$

The answers are on the next page

Key Stage 3 Maths Explained - Volume 2 Algebra

Answers to Exercise 2

1) $y = 14$

2) $y = 41$

3) $y = 11$

4) $y = 27$

5) $y = 60$

6) $y = 17$

7) $y = 13$

8) $y = 24$

9) $y = 38$

10) $y = 34$

Chapter 3 – Powers

Powers are another basic idea. Suppose you want to multiply letters by numbers, or letters by letters? Suppose you want to add letters together or subtract one from another?

It is not difficult!

        Suppose you have 3 × 9   easy   3 × 9 = 27

        Suppose you have 3 × **a**   easy, 3 × **a** is written as 3**a**

        Suppose you have **a** × **a**   that is also easy! So, read on.

You have a square and its sides are **a** cm long:

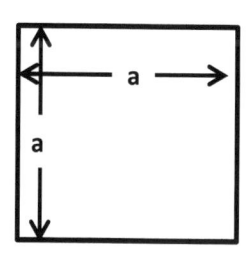

The area of this square is **a** × **a**.
So, we say **a** × **a** = **a** squared
and write **a** × **a** as **a**^{2}.
The little 2 is called an index.
a^2 is an easy way of writing **a** × **a**.

Figure 1

The volume of this cube is **a** × **a** × **a** = **a**^{3}.
So, we say **a**^{3} = **a** cubed.

Fortunately, those are the only special names as **a** × **a** × **a** × **a** × **a** = **a**^{5} is just called "**a** to the fifth"

a × **a** × **a** × **a** × **a** × **a** × **a** = **a**^{7}
is "**a** to the seventh" and so on.

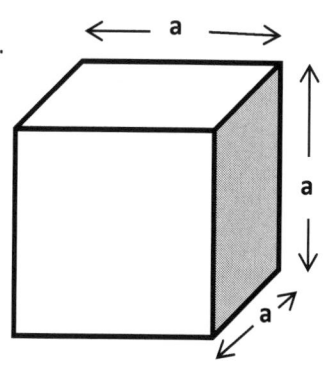

Figure 2

Key Stage 3 Maths Explained - Volume 2 Algebra

So, a = a,   a × a = a²,   a × a × a = a³,   a × a × a × a = a⁴

Each time you add an extra 'a' to the string you add 1 to the small, raised number. This number is called the **power (or index) and** tells you how many letter a's are to be multiplied together.

Suppose you have $2x^3$
The power (that is the small 3), only applies to the x.

So $2x^3 = 2 \times x^3 = 2 \times x \times x \times x$.

If you want the 2 to be to be cubed as well, that is $2 \times 2 \times 2 \times x \times x \times x$ then you put brackets round the $2x$ and the cubed sign outside the brackets.

$(2x)^3 = 2 \times 2 \times 2 \times x \times x \times x$

So $2x^3 = 2 \times x \times x \times x$, and $2^3 x = 2 \times 2 \times 2 \times x$.
and $(2x)^3 = 2x \times 2x \times 2x$

Unless there are brackets round the term, the power only applies to the letter or number immediately before it.

$3x \times y^3 = 3 \times x \times (y \times y \times y) = 3xy^3$

$3(x^3)\, y = 3 \times (x \times x \times x) \times y = 3x^3 y$
$3^3 xy = (3 \times 3 \times 3) \times x \times y = 3^3\, xy = 9\, xy$
$3(xy)^3 = 3 \times (x \times y) \times (x \times y) \times (x \times y) = 3x^3 y^3$
$(3xy)^3 = (3 \times x \times y) \times (3 \times x \times y) \times (3 \times x \times y)$
$\qquad = 3^3 \times x^3 \times y^3 = 27x^3 y^3$

The brackets show exactly what is being cubed.

Chapter 3 – Powers

In the answer to a question you would write:
$3xy^3$, $3x^3y$, 3^3xy, $3(xy)^3$, or $3x^3y^3$

The power only applies to the letter or number immediately before it, unless the power is outside a bracket. If it is immediately outside a bracket, it applies to everything which is inside the bracket:

So $(xy)^3 = (xy) \times (xy) \times (xy)$
$= x \times y \times x \times y \times x \times y$
$= x^3 \times y^3$

Exercise 3

Expand these expressions, for example $9x^2y = 9 \times x \times x \times y$
(The term **expression** is used for any short piece of algebra)

Q1 1) x^3 2) x^4 3) x^2 4) x^5 5) x^6

Q2. 1) bx^2 2) ax^3 3) a^2x^3 4) b^3x^2 5) b^3x

Q3 1) $(bx)^2$ 2) $3(bx)^2$ 3) $3(bx)^3$ 4) $(3bx)^2$ 5) $(4bx^2)^2$

The answers are on the next page.

Key Stage 3 Maths Explained - Volume 2 Algebra

Answers to Exercise 3

Q1 1) $x \times x \times x$ 2) $x \times x \times x \times x$

3) $x \times x$ 4) $x \times x \times x \times x \times x$

5) $x \times x \times x \times x \times x \times x$

Q2. 1) $b \times x \times x$ 2) $a \times x \times x \times x$

3) $a \times a \times x \times x \times x$ 4) $b \times b \times b \times x \times x$

5) $b \times b \times b \times x$

Q3 1) $b \times b \times x \times x$ 2) $3 \times b \times b \times x \times x$

3) $3 \times b \times b \times b \times x \times x \times x$ 4) $3 \times 3 \times b \times b \times x \times x$

5) $4 \times 4 \times b \times b \times x \times x \times x \times x$

Chapter 4 - Roots

Roots are the opposite of powers.

If you have $x^2 = x \times x$ then x is the square root of x^2. So, finding the square root is finding the original number; that is number which was squared to give x^2. The sign for the square root is $\sqrt{}$.

This sign is used for the **square root**, $\sqrt{x^2} = x$.

If you want the **cube root** you write $\sqrt[3]{x^3} = x$

For the fourth root you write $\sqrt[4]{x^4} = x$, and so on.

The cube root of $x^3 = x$

x	$x \times x = x^2$	$x \times x \times x = x^3$
2	2 × 2 = 4	2 × 2 × 2 = 8
3	3 × 3 = 9	3 × 3 × 3 = 27
4	4 × 4 = 16	4 × 4 × 4 = 64
5	5 × 5 = 25	5 × 5 × 5 = 125

Writing this the other way round

$$x = \sqrt{x^2} \text{ or } x = \sqrt[3]{x^3}$$

x^2	$x = \sqrt{x^2}$	x^3	$x = \sqrt[3]{x^3}$
4	2	8	2
9	3	27	3
16	4	64	4
25	5	125	5

If $x^2 = 4$, then as 4 = 2 × 2 and $x^2 = x \times x$ then $x = 2$
If $x^2 = 9$, then as 9 = 3 × 3 and $x^2 = x \times x$ then $x = 3$
If $x^2 = 16$, then as 16 = 4 × 4 and $x^2 = x \times x$ then $x = 4$
If $x^2 = 25$, then as 25 = 5 × 5 and $x^2 = x \times x$ then $x = 5$

Key Stage 3 Maths Explained - Volume 2 Algebra

The same thing happens with cube roots:

If $x^3 = 8$, then as $8 = 2 \times 2 \times 2$ and $x^3 = x \times x \times x$ then $x = 2$
If $x^3 = 27$ then as $27 = 3 \times 3 \times 3$ and $x^3 = x \times x \times x$ then $x = 3$
If $x^3 = 64$ then as $64 = 4 \times 4 \times 4$ and $x^3 = x \times x \times x$ then $x = 4$
If $x^3 = 125$, then as $125 = 5 \times 5 \times 5$ and $x^3 = x \times x \times x$ then $x = 5$

There are a lot of numbers in chapters 3 and 4. They are there to illustrate and help to explain the ideas in algebra. Although we treat the sections of maths as though they are totally separate, there are places where you have to use them together.

A tip from your tutor

You will find a detailed account of using square roots and cube roots in Chapters 36 and 37 of Maths? Don't Panic Volume 1, "Arithmetic"

Here I am going to look at another way of writing square roots and cube roots. This makes things easier.

The square root of 4 can be written as $4^{1/2}$ and the cube root as $4^{1/3}$.

So, you have 4^3, 4^2, 4^1, $4^{1/2}$, $4^{1/3}$. They are all powers of 4. They are based on 4^1 which is simply 4. The squares cubes and so on are all bigger than 4. When the powers get smaller, the value of that power of four gets smaller.

Here is a table of powers of 4 from 4^5 to $4^{1/5}$, with their values

Power of 4	4^5	4^4	4^3	4^2	4	$4^{1/2}$	$4^{1/3}$	$4^{1/4}$	$4^{1/5}$
Numerical value	1024	256	64	16	4	2	1.587	1.4142	1.3195

Chapter 4 - Roots

So, you can see that this is a long series.
If the page was wide enough we could go from:
$4^{100} = (1{\cdot}606938044 \times 10^{60})$ to $4^{1/100} = 4^{0.01} = (1{\cdot}01395948)$. If you do this you end up with long strings of numbers, and very complicated numbers they are. Using powers is much easier and they work for a whole range of numbers. You can now deal with powers and roots.

$2 \times 2 = 4$	therefor $4 = 2 \times 2$	2 is a factor of 4
$2^2 = 4$	2 squared is 4	So $2 = \sqrt{4} = 4^{1/2}$
$3 \times 3 = 3^2 = 9$	3 squared = 9	So $3 = \sqrt{9} = 9^{1/2}$
$2 \times 2 \times 2 = 8$	$8 = 2^3$	So $2 = 8^{1/3}$
$3 \times 3 \times 3 = 27$	$27 = 3^3$	So $3 = 27^{1/3}$
$2 \times 2 \times 2 \times 2 = 16$	Therefor $16 = 2^4$	So $2 = 16^{1/4}$
$3 \times 3 \times 3 \times 3 = 81$	Therefor $81 = 3^4$	So $3 = 81^{1/4}$

Exercise 4

Write them out as above but you may use a calculator to work out the numbers.
To find x^5 when $x = 6$ which is $6^5 = 6 \times 6 \times 6 \times 6 \times 6 = 7776$.
On your calculator press 6 then □ and then 5 (or do exactly what your calculator booklet tells you to do.)

1) Find: a) 5^3, b) 4^4, c) 3^5, d) 2^6 e) 3^3, f) 4^6 g) 5^5

2) Using a calculator, find the following roots.
(To find $10^{1/2}$ using a calculator, enter 10 then $x^{\square}$ (or x^y), then $1 \div 2$ you will get $3{\cdot}16227766$)

a) $9^{1/2}$ b) $16^{1/4}$ c) $25^{1/2}$ d) $8^{1/3}$ e) $27^{1/3}$ f) $64^{1/3}$ g) $125^{1/3}$

For h) to n) give your answers to 3 decimal places.
h) $11^{1/2}$ i) $13^{1/3}$ j) $15^{1/43}$ k) $7^{1/3}$ l) $11^{1/3}$ m) $17^{1/9}$ n) $23^{1/4}$

Key Stage 3 Maths Explained - Volume 2 Algebra

Answers to Exercise 4

1) a) 125   b) 256   c) 243   d) 64   e) 27

   f) 4096   g) 3125.

2) a) 3   b) 2   c) 5   d) 2

   e) 3   f) 4   g) 4   h) 3·317

   i) 2·351   j) 1·968   k) 2·646   l) 2·224

   m) 1·370   n) 2·190

Chapter 5 Powers and Reciprocals

Powers and Reciprocals.

This is a very easy chapter. The **reciprocal** of 5 is $\frac{1}{5}$. The reciprocal of a number is 1 divided by the number. This applies in algebra as well. The reciprocal of x is $\frac{1}{x}$. The reciprocal of $2x$ is $\frac{1}{2x}$

To show this as a **power** is quite simple $\frac{1}{x} = x^{-1}$.

You can think of this as rearranging:

The x moves up and the — $\frac{1}{x} = x^{-1}$

(the line between the 1 and the x) becomes -1

So, the reciprocal of any algebraic function is: $\frac{1}{\text{function}}$

The reciprocal of $2x^3$ is $\frac{1}{2x^3}$, or $(2x^3)^{-1}$. **The brackets ( )** round the $2x^3$ show that the bracket is treated a packet. When you have a power outside a bracket it applies to **everything** in the bracket but **not** to anything outside the bracket:

$(3x)^2 = 3x \times 3x = 9x^2$

$3(x)^2 = 3 \times x^2 = 3x^2 = 3 \times x \times x$

$3(x)^{-2} = 3 \times x^{-2} = 3 \times \frac{1}{x} \times \frac{1}{x} = \frac{3}{x^2} = \frac{3}{x \times x}$

$(3x)^{-2} = \frac{1}{(3x)^2} = \frac{1}{3x \times 3x} = \frac{1}{9x^2}$

Key Stage 3 Maths Explained   Volume 2 Algebra

Powers, a summary

The reciprocal of x is x^{-1} which equals $\dfrac{1}{x}$.

The square of x is x^2 which equals $x \times x$.

The square root of x is $x^{1/2}$ which equals $\sqrt{x}$

A tip from your tutor

You need to be very careful with brackets. If you have a power outside a bracket then that power applies to everything in the bracket, but not to anything outside the bracket.

$5(3 + 3x)^2 = 5 \times (3 + 3x)^2 = 5 \times (3 + 3x) \times (3 + 3x)$

$5^2(3 + 3x)^2 = 5 \times 5 \times (3 + 3x) \times (3 + 3x)$

$5^2(3 + 3x) = 5 \times 5 \times (3 + 3x)$

Powers are very useful, they save lots of time and writing. Use them carefully and they will save you time and marks.

Chapter 5   Powers and Reciprocals

Exercise 5

Expand these expressions.

1) $(5y)^2$, $(7x)^3$, $(2z)^4$, $(3y)^3$

2) $6(x)^2$, $5(y)^3$, $4(z)^2$, $7(x)^4$

3) $2(z)^{-3}$, $4(x)^{-2}$, $7(z)^{-1}$, $8(y)^{-3}$,

4) $(4x)^{-1}$, $(5x)^{-2}$ $(2y)^{-3}$ $(3x)^{-4}$

5) $9^{1/2}$, $4^{1/2}$, $16^{1/2}$, $27^{1/3}$, $8^{1/3}$, $64^{1/3}$,

6) $3(x+2)^2$, $6(x-1)^2$, $7(2x+4)^2$, $8(3x-1)^2$,

7) $4^2(x+2)$, $3^3(x-1)$, $2^3(x+3)$, $3^2(x-3)$,

8) $2^2(x+1)^2$, $4^2(x-1)^2$, $3^3(x+2)^2$, $2^3(x-3)^3$,

The answers are on the next page.

Key Stage 3 Maths Explained   Volume 2 Algebra

Answers to Exercise 5

1) $25y^2$ $343x^3$ $16z^4$ $27y^3$

2) $6x^2$ $5y^3$ $4z^2$ $7x^4$

3) $\dfrac{2}{z^3}$ $\dfrac{4}{x^2}$ $\dfrac{7}{z}$ $\dfrac{8}{y^3}$

4) $\dfrac{1}{4x}$ $\dfrac{1}{25x^2}$ $\dfrac{1}{8y^3}$ $\dfrac{1}{81x^4}$

5) 3, 2, 4, 3, 2, 4,

6) $3x^2 + 12x + 12$, $6x^2 - 12x + 6$,

   $28x^2 + 112x + 112$, $72x^2 - 48x + 1$

7) $16x + 32$ $27x - 27$ $8x + 24$ $9x - 27$

8) $4x^2 + 8x + 4$, $16x^2 - 32x + 16$, $27x^2 + 108x + 108$,

   $8x^3 - 72x^2 + 261x - 216$,

Chapter 6   Linear Equations

Some equations, are a bit more difficult. Don't, worry; they are only slightly more difficult! The first equations were very easy.

You were given the equation $y = x + 3$ and told: If $x = 5$, find the value of y.
So, you put $x = 5$ and got $y = 5 + 3$ so $y = 8$.

This is a linear equation. Now with a number in front of the x

The next step is also simple. Suppose $y = 2x + 5$; what is the value of y?

As $2x = 2 \times x$; this is easy. If $x = 6$ then:

$y = 2x + 5$
$= 2 \times 6 + 5$
$= 12 + 5$
$= 17$

Remember, multiply before adding

The next step is equally easy.

If $2y = 3x + 4$, and $x = 6$, what is y?

Write the equation	Step 1)	$2y = 3x + 4$
	Step 2)	$2y = 3 \times x + 4$
Put 6 for x	Step 3)	$2y = 3 \times 6 + 4$
So,	Step 4)	$2y = 18 + 4$
Add up the right hand side,	Step 5)	$2y = 22$
Divide both sides by 2	Step 6)	$y = 11$

The extra step is the "divide both sides by 2" in line 6. This is obvious. If 2 cakes cost 22p then 1 will cost 11p. So, if $2y = 22$, $y = 11$.

Key Stage 3 Maths Explained   Volume 2 Algebra

Here is another example:

If $3y = 4x + 5$, find y when $x = 16$

Step 1) $x = 16,$
Step 2)   so $4 \times x = 4 \times 16 = 64$
Step 3) $3y = 4x + 5 = 64 + 5$
Step 4) $3y = 69$
Step 5) $y = \dfrac{69}{3}$ $3 \overline{)69}^{\,23}$
Step 6) Then $y = \dfrac{69}{3} = 23$

A tip from your tutor

Do keep the calculations, like (16 × 4 and 69 ÷ 3) within your working.

There are five reasons for doing this.
1) It helps you get the right answer.
2) If you get the answer wrong, it is easy to look for, find, and correct your mistake.
3) When you revise for exams you can see quickly exactly how you got to the right answer.
4) You soon remember the whole process.
5) You must do this in examinations to get full marks. You don't get full marks if you don't show your working

If it takes time to do these calculations, get out your calculator, switch it on, enter the numbers, and then copy the answer. Remember that calculators give the right answer to the calculation you entered. You can make a mistake entering the number or copying the answer. Calculators must be used with care. They do exactly what you tell them to do! So, it is still up to you to get the right answer: and to spot the wrong one!

Chapter 6   Linear Equations

Exercise 6. Now try these questions:

1. If $y = 2x + 4$, find the value of y

when $x =$ a) 5,   b) 9,   c) 3,   d) 6,   e) 11

2. If $y = 3x - 6$, find the value of y

when $x =$ a) 4,   b) 7,   c) 12,   d) 3,   e) 15

3. If $3y = 6x + 9$, find the value of y

when $x =$ a) 2,   b) 5,   c) 7,   d) 9,   e) 14

4. If $4y = 12x + 8$, find the value of y

when $x =$ a) 6,   b) 9,   c) 7,   d) 3,   e) 5

The answers are on the next page.

Key Stage 3 Maths Explained   Volume 2 Algebra

Answers to Exercise 6

1) a) 14,   b) 22,   c) 10,   d) 16,   e) 26

2) a) 6,   b) 15,   c) 30,   d) 3,   e) 39

3) a) 7,   b) 13,   c) 17,   d) 21,   e) 31

4) a) 20,   b) 29,   c) 23,   d) 11,   e) 17

Chapter 7 Brackets

Brackets are like plastic bags. They hold several things together so that you can move them as a group.

For example: you buy 3 apples, 2 oranges, 2 bananas and a pineapple. Without a plastic bag to put them in you would have problems carrying them home. Put them in a plastic bag and it's easy.

In algebra you can say. $\dfrac{3}{5x + 3y} = 4$

If you put the $5x + 3y$ in brackets, $\dfrac{3}{(5x+ 3y)} = 4$

That is like putting the $5x + 3y$ into a plastic bag. Then you can move the bracket, as you would a plastic bag of fruit, to the other side of the equals sign. $\dfrac{3}{(5x+ 3y)} = 4$ becomes $3 = 4 \times (5x + 3y)$

This goes further. You have four plastic bags each holding 5 apples and 3 bananas. That is four bags or 4 × (5 apples + 3 bananas). If you empty out the bags you have 4 × 5 = 20 apples and 4 × 3 = 12 bananas. For short write **a** for apple and **b** for bananas. Then you have:

4 × (5a + 3b)

To start with you had 4 × (5a + 3b).
So common sense tells you that 4 × (5a + 3b) = 20a + 12b, Twenty apple and twelve bananas.

Key Stage 3 Maths Explained   Volume 2 Algebra

There is no difference in maths. Maths must be based on common sense! So, to expand a bracket, multiply everything in the bracket by the number outside the bracket.

$6(3x + 2) \quad = 6 \times 3x + 6 \times 2$
$ = 18x + 12$

$5(3x + 6) \quad = 5 \times 3x + 5 \times 6$
$ = 15x + 30$

If you have a negative sign inside the bracket you use the same method but use the negative sign when you multiply.

$7(4x - 3) \quad = 7 \times 4x - 7 \times 3$
$ = 28x - 21$

$4(2x - 4) \quad = 4 \times 2x - 4 \times 4$
$ = 8x - 16$

Now try exercise 7 on the next page.

Chapter 7 Brackets

Exercise 7

Expand the following brackets.

1) $3(4x - 5)$ 2) $2(3x + 6)$ 3) $6(5x - 2)$

4) $4(7x + 2)$ 5) $7(2x - 6)$ 6) $5(6x + 3)$

7) $9(8x - 4)$ 8) $6(3x + 4)$ 9) $11(2x + 5)$

10) $3(3x - 2)$ 11) $9(4x + 7)$ 12) $7(9x - 5)$

The answers are on the next page

Key Stage 3 Maths Explained   Volume 2 Algebra

Answers to Exercise 7

1) $12x - 15$

2) $6x + 12$

3) $30x - 12$

4) $28x + 8$

5) $14x - 42$

6) $30x + 15$

7) $72x - 36$

8) $18x + 24$

9).. $22x + 55$

10) $9x - 6$

11) $36x + 63$

12) $63x - 35$

Chapter 8 – Graphs, Axes and Points

To plot graphs, you need to have numbers on the graph

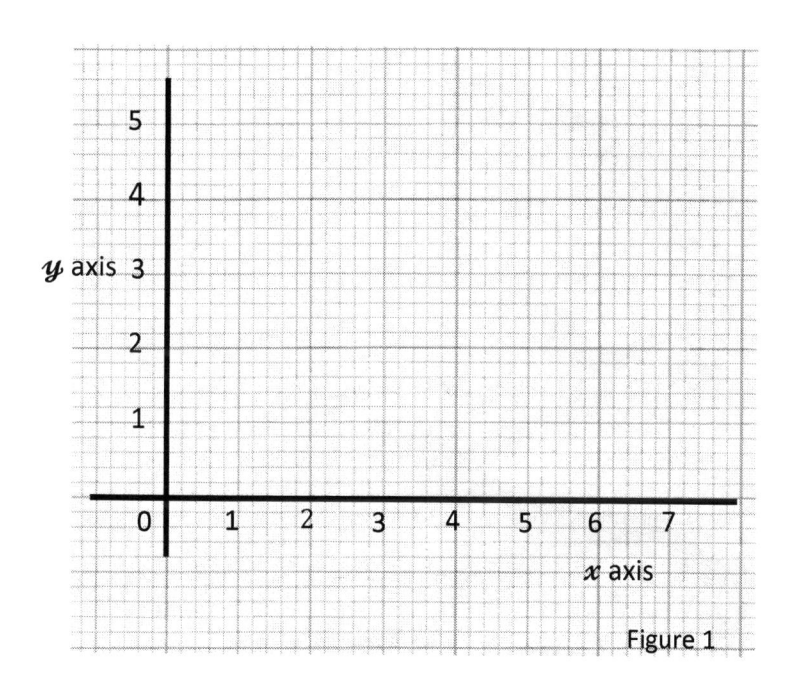

Figure 1

As an example, here the x axis is labelled with the numbers 1 to 7.

The y axis is labelled with the numbers 1 to 5.

Key Stage 3 Maths Explained   Volume 2 Algebra

Putting points on the graph is simple.

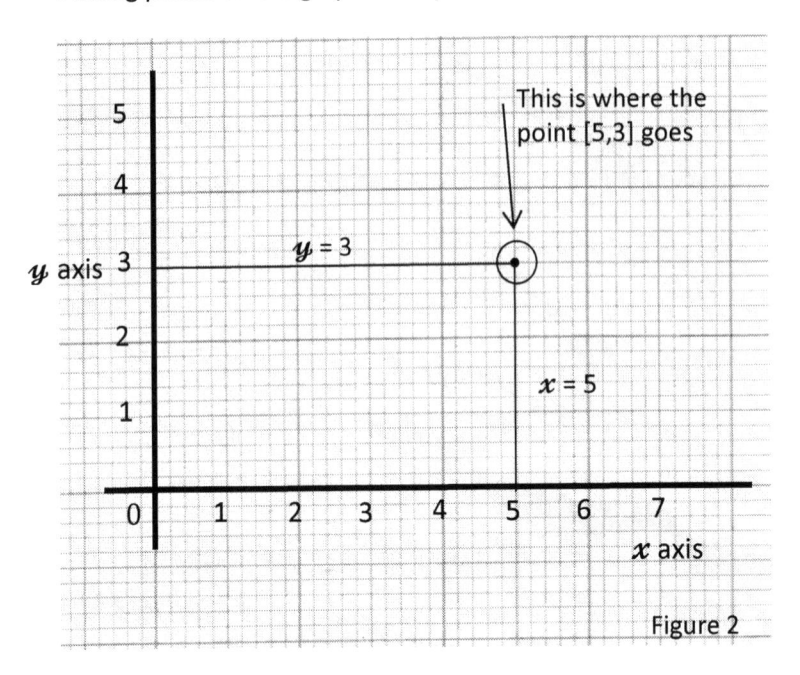

Figure 2

If you are asked to plot the point [5,3] for example, this means the point where x = 5 and y = 3. The square brackets show that the two letters or numbers are the **coordinates** of a point. The value of x is always written first, then a comma, and then the y.
Start at the **origin.**
(The origin is the point 0 on the bottom left of the graph where the axes cross).

x = 5 so the point will be somewhere on the line going up from x = 5. The value of y is 3. So the point will be somewhere on the line going across from y = 3 the point you were asked to plot was [5,3]: so it must be where the lines cross on the diagram. The point is marked with a dot and has a ring drawn round it as in figure 2.

(There is no exercise on this chapter)

Chapter 9 – Plotting Graphs

Plotting Graphs. If you can plot one point you can plot several and draw a line through them.

Figure 3 is a set of graphs which show how the value of y can change with the value of x. You can look at the graph and find the value of y for any value of x. Now look at the equations $y = x$, $y = 2x$, $y = 3x$, and $y = 4x$.

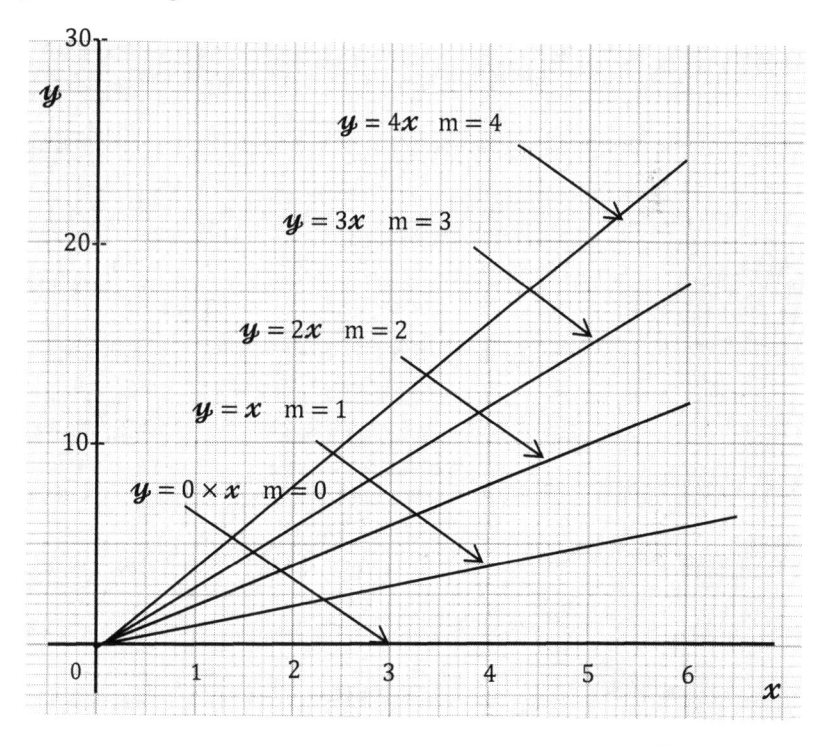

$y = 4x \quad m = 4$

$y = 3x \quad m = 3$

$y = 2x \quad m = 2$

$y = x \quad m = 1$

$y = 0 \times x \quad m = 0$

Figure 3

As you can see, the slopes (or gradients) of the graphs increase as the number in front of the x increases. So, to describe the line completely a measure of the gradient must be included in the equation of the line.

The letter **m is used for the gradient**. The gradient or slope of the line is measured by comparing the horizontal and vertical distances it traces. The graph shows that when the line passes through the origin the equation of the line is y = mx.

In the graph of $y = x$ the values of y are equal to the values of x. So as $y = x$ and $y = mx$, m must be equal to 1.

In the graph of $y = 2x$, m = 2. In the graph of $y = 3x$, m = 3. In the graph of $y = 4x$, m = 4. So, m is the number which multiplies x in the equation: and it measures the slope or gradient of the line.

You will see that the x axis itself has m = 0. So, all the values of y are 0, as 0 × (any number) = 0.

Exercise 9 is on the next page

Chapter 9 – Plotting Graphs

Exercise 9

On an A5 sheet of graph paper draw the x and y axes as shown in figure 3. Label the y axis from 0 to 40 and the x axis from 0 to 7. Make a table showing the value of y for each value of x when x = 1, 2, 3, 4, 5, 6, 7
Plot the lines:

1) $y = 1{\cdot}5x$, 2) $y = 2{\cdot}5x$, 3) $y = 5x$,

4) $y = 3x$, 5) $y = 4x$, 6) $y = 6x$

The answers are on the next page

Key Stage 3 Maths Explained   Volume 2 Algebra

Answers to Exercise 9

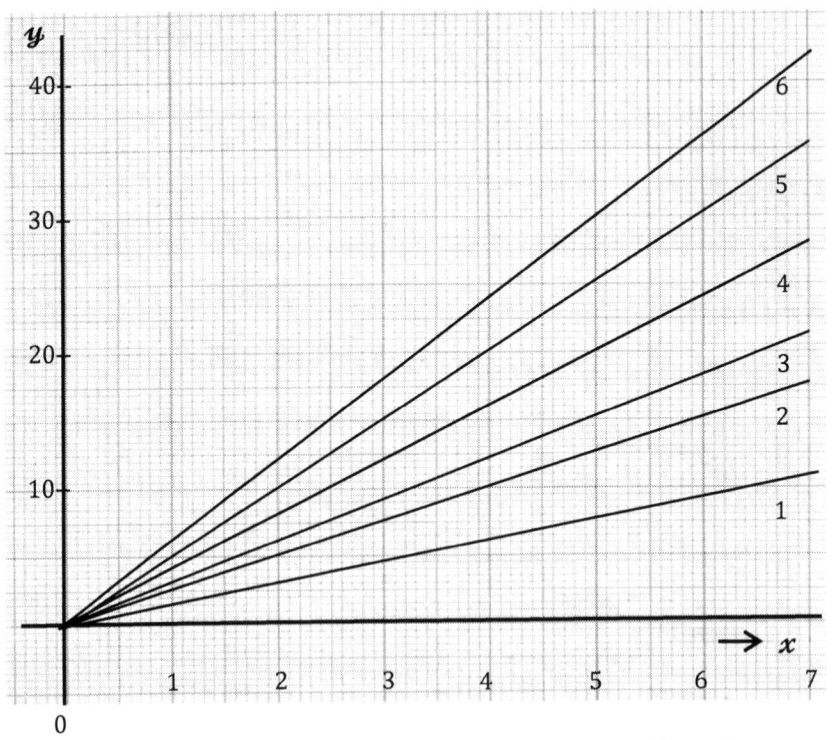

Figure 4

	Equation	$x =$	1	2	3	4	5	6	7
1	$y = 1 \cdot 5\,x$	$y =$	1·5	3	4·5	6	7·5	9	10·5
2	$y = 2 \cdot 5\,x$	$y =$	2·5	5	7·5	10	12·5	15	17·5
3	$y = 3\,x$	$y =$	3	6	9	12	15	18	21
4	$y = 4\,x$	$y =$	4	8	12	16	20	24	28
5	$y = 5\,x$	$y =$	5	10	15	20	25	30	35
6	$y = 6\,x$	$y =$	6	12	18	24	30	36	42

Chapter 10 - Straight Line Graphs

Straight Line Graphs

So far, we have drawn lines that have the equation $y = mx$ and they all went through the origin. So now let's look at some lines that all have the same slope (m = 1) but cross the y axis at different points. Let's plot graphs for $y = mx + c$, where c can be 1, 2, 3, 4, 5, or 6.

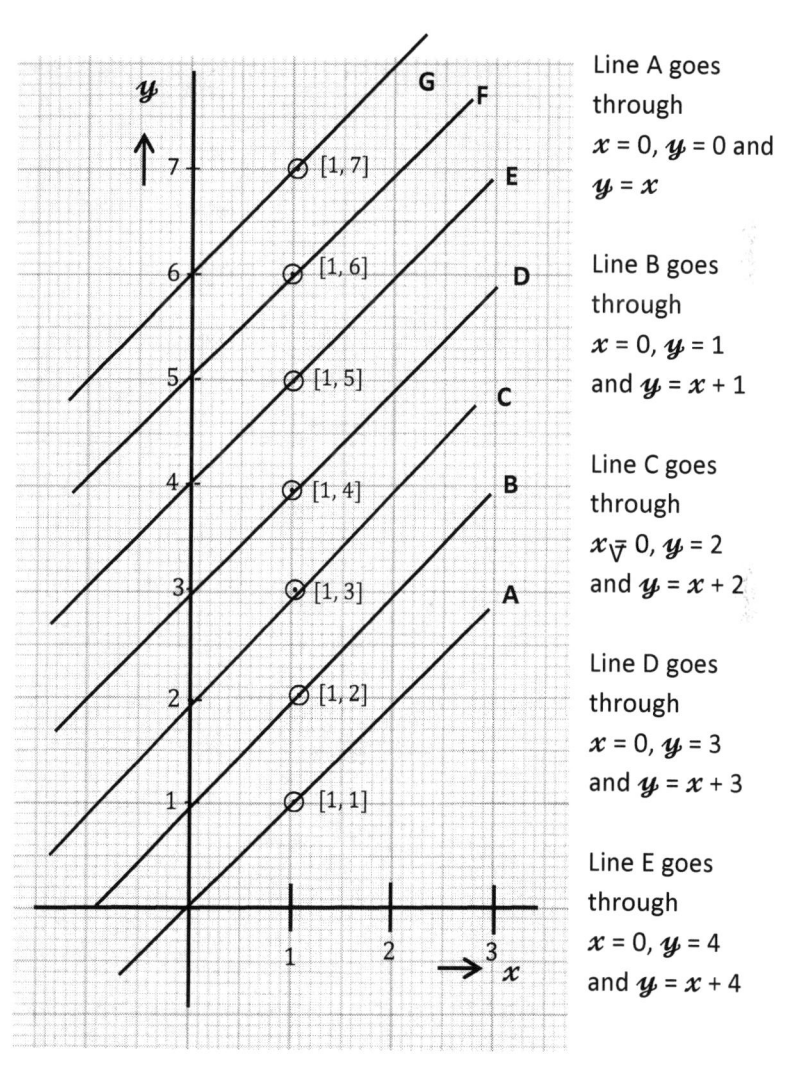

Line A goes through $x = 0$, $y = 0$ and $y = x$

Line B goes through $x = 0$, $y = 1$ and $y = x + 1$

Line C goes through $x = 0$, $y = 2$ and $y = x + 2$

Line D goes through $x = 0$, $y = 3$ and $y = x + 3$

Line E goes through $x = 0$, $y = 4$ and $y = x + 4$

Line F goes through $x = 0$, $y = 5$ and $y = x + 5$
Line G goes through $x = 0$, $y = 6$ and $y = x + 6$.

Key Stage 3 Maths Explained - Volume 2 Algebra

So now we can change the formula to show where the line crosses the x axis. The full formula is:

$$y = mx + c$$

The 'm' is the slope or gradient of the line and the 'c' is where it crosses the y axis.

Now you can draw any straight-line graph.

If $y = 3x + 4$, then when $x = 0$, $y = 4$, it crosses the y axis at $y = 4$.

When $x = 2$ then $y = 3 \times 2 + 4 = 10$.
So, it goes through the point [2,10].

When $x = 4$ then $y = 3 \times 4 + 4 = 16$.
So, it goes through the point [4,16].

Using this kind of formula, you can draw any straight line on a graph. By putting $x = 0$ you can find where the line crosses the y axis. By putting $y = 0$ you can find where the line crosses the x axis.

So, in the equation $y = 3x + 4$, when $y = 0$, $3x + 4 = 0$ so $x = -\frac{4}{3}$
and the line goes through the point $[-\frac{4}{3}, 0]$.

In other words, if you are given the formula, you can put points on the graph paper and draw the straight line described by the formula.

Chapter 10 - Straight Line Graphs

Exercise 10

Make a table of the values of y when:

1) $y = 2x + 3$ for values of x from 0 to 6

2) $y = 3x + 1$ for values of x from 0 to 6

3) $y = 2x - 2$ for values of x from 0 to 6

Then plot the graphs.

The answers are on the next page

Key Stage 3 Maths Explained - Volume 2 Algebra

Answers to Exercise 10

1) $y = 2x + 3$

x	$2x$	$2x + 3$
0	0	3
1	2	5
2	4	7
3	6	9
4	8	11
5	10	13
6	12	15

2) $y = 3x + 1$

x	$3x$	$3x + 1$
0	0	1
1	3	4
2	6	7
3	9	10
4	12	13
5	15	16
6	18	19

3) $y = 2x - 2$

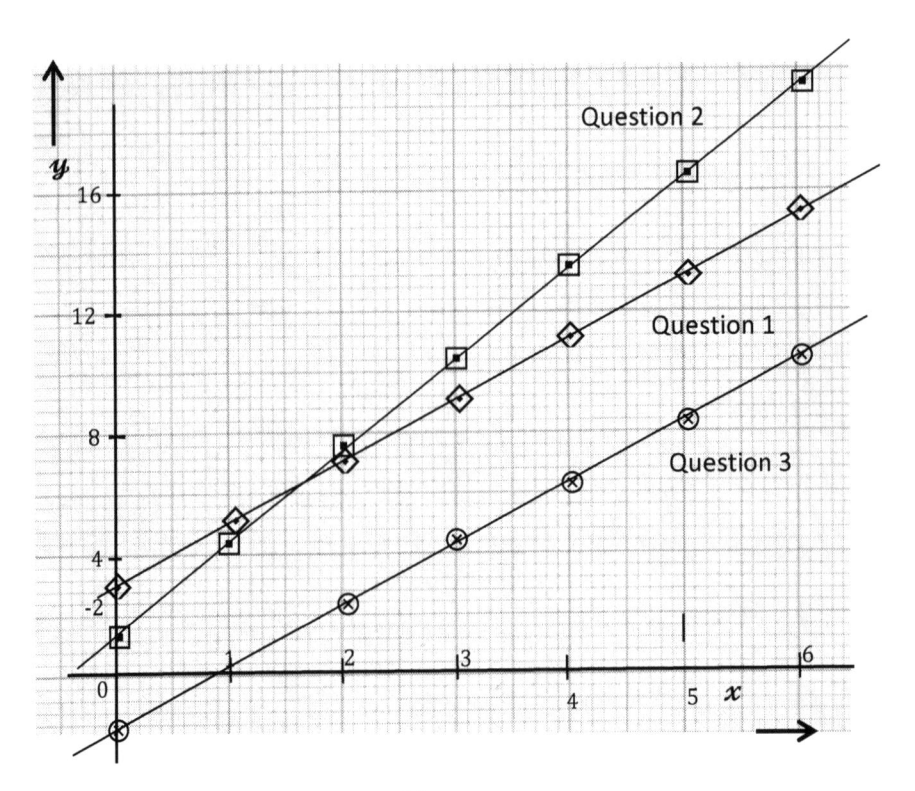

x	$2x$	$2x - 2$
0	0	-2
1	2	0
2	4	2
3	6	4
4	8	6
5	10	8
6	12	10

Chapter 11 - Lines with Negative Slopes

Lines with negative slopes.

Chapters 9 and 10 looked at lines which go from lower left to upper right. Now look at these lines which go from upper left to lower right.

The axes will be exactly the same, and have exactly the same numbers on them, but the graph will go from top left to bottom right like the graph in Figure 1.

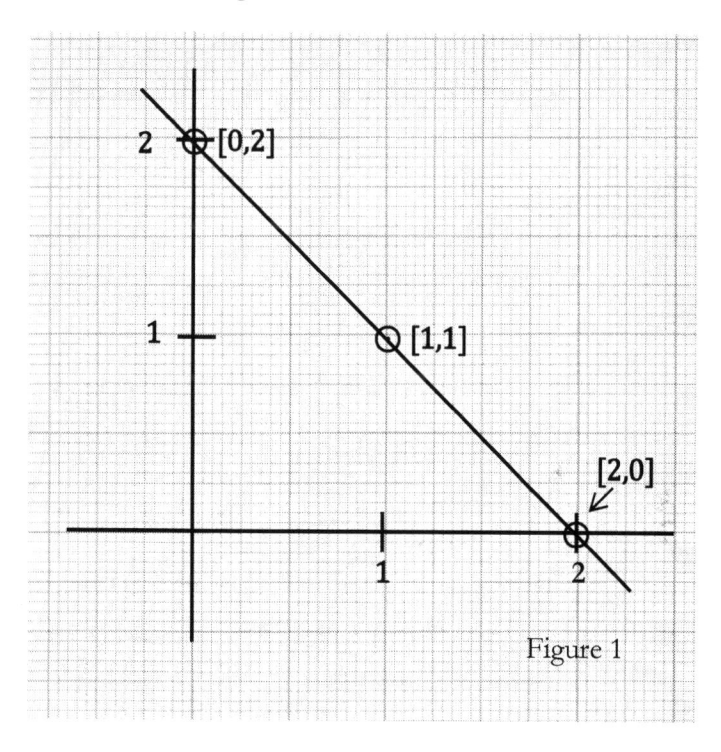

Figure 1

This means that as x gets bigger y gets smaller.
The three points on the graph are [0, 2]; [1, 1]; [2, 0].
The values of x are 0, 1, 2 so they are obviously getting bigger.
The values of y are 2, 1, 0; obviously getting smaller.
So, the gradient of the graph is, as before.

$$\frac{\text{Change in } y}{\text{Change in } x} = \frac{-2 \text{(It goes down from 2 to 0)}}{+2 \text{ (It goes up from 0 to2)}} = \frac{-2}{+2} = -1$$

Key Stage 3 Maths Explained - Volume 2 Algebra

Graphs with negative slopes obey all the rules given in chapters 9 and 10, and you treat them in exactly the same way. You just have to remember that as x gets bigger y gets smaller, and the lines slope the other way. Provided you draw diagrams and label them carefully you should find negative slopes no more difficult than positive ones. Just remember these diagrams.

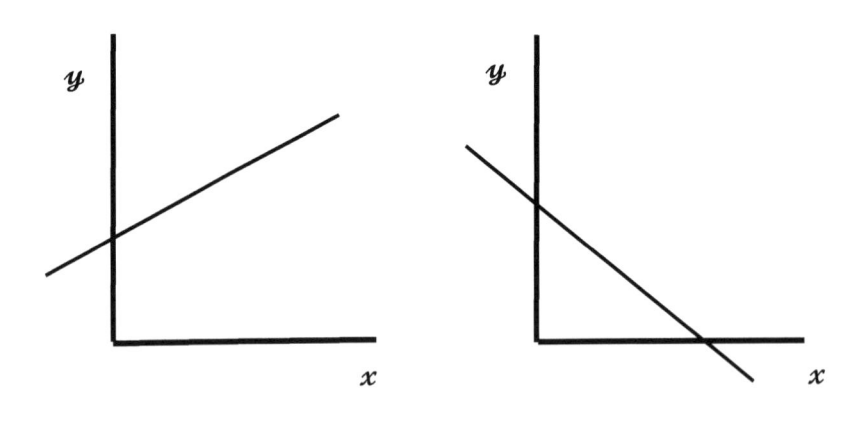

Positive slope or
gradient m is +
y gets bigger
as x gets bigger

Negative slope or
gradient m is −
y gets smaller
as x gets bigger

There is no exercise on this chapter

Chapter 12 – Horizontal Lines, Vertical Lines and Quadrants

Horizontal and Vertical Lines

Some graphs have lines that are horizontal, they show that y is always equal to 1 (or 2 or 3) for every value of x.

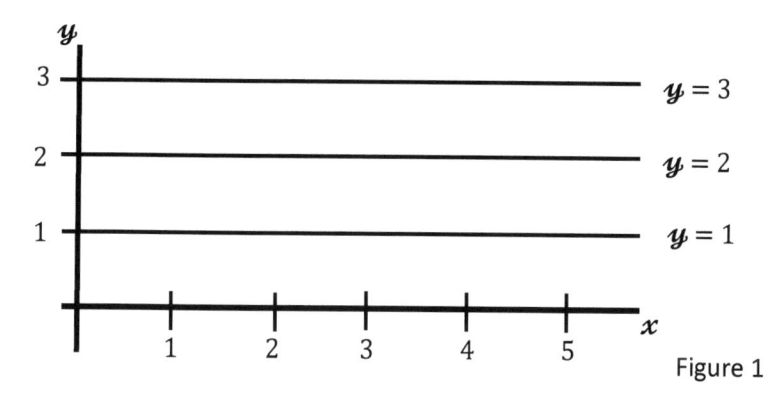

Figure 1

So, the equations for these graphs are simply $y = a\ number$. As there is no x term the constant is all that is left.

If the lines are vertical they are showing that the equations are: $x = 2$, $x = 4$, $x = 6$. There is no y in these equations so the equation is again very simple, and no constant is required (as the lines never cross the y axis).

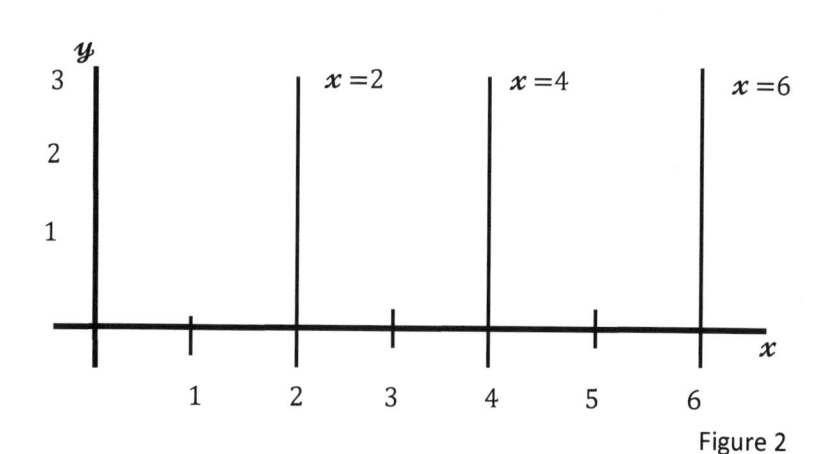

Figure 2

43

Key Stage 3 Maths Explained - Volume 2 Algebra

So far, all the graphs we have drawn have had both x and y as positive numbers. This is the most usual way in which graphs are drawn.

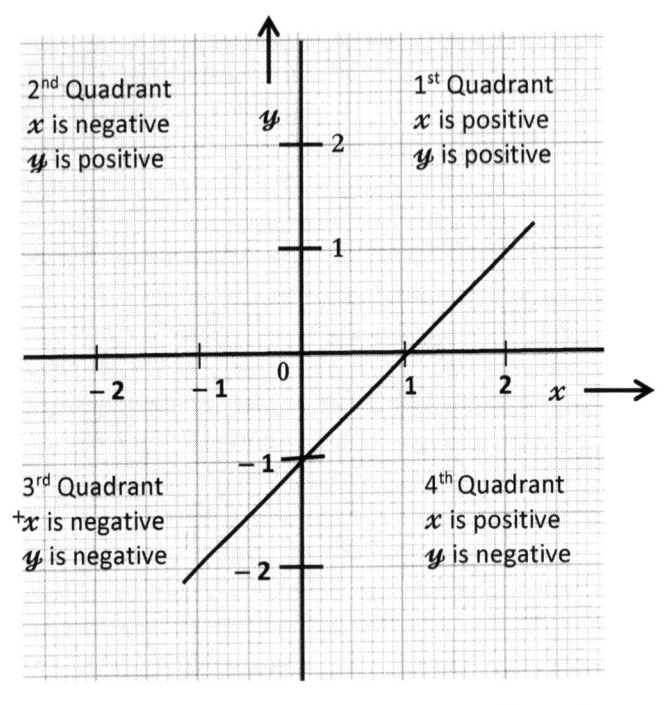

Figure 3

A graph can however be drawn with up to four **quadrants** if necessary.

The line shown in this graph has the equation $y = x - 1$. It goes from the third quadrant, where both x and y are negative, through the fourth quadrant, where x is positive and y is negative and into the first quadrant where both x and y are positive.

There is no exercise on this chapter.

Chapter 13 – Sequences or Series

Sequences or series are lists of numbers which have a regular pattern: two different names for the same thing.

The simplest series is 1,2,3,4,5,6,7.

Here the pattern is obvious. To get to the next number you add 1. You call this counting! So, you are already quite happy with it. Each number is 1 bigger than the previous number, and 1 less than the number which comes after it. This type of series is called an **arithmetic series** because you add or subtract a number to get from one term to another

Here are two other examples: 2, 4, 6, 8, and 5, 10, 15, 20.

Before you know exactly what to write down you must know **three** things about the series:

    1) Which number to start with.
    2) How much you must add, or subtract, to get
        from one number to the next,
    3) When to stop.

So, you could be asked to start with 2 and by adding 2 find a list of 10 numbers.

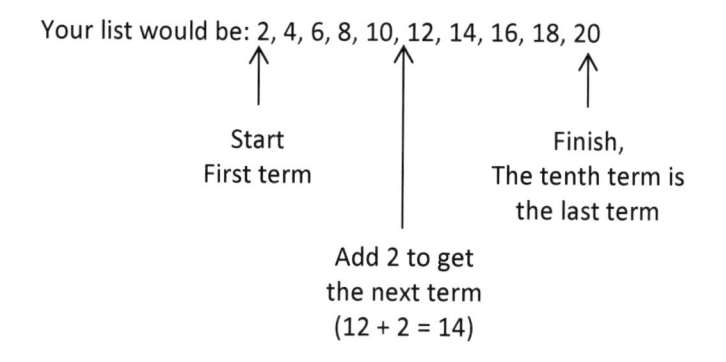

Your list would be: 2, 4, 6, 8, 10, 12, 14, 16, 18, 20

↑   ↑   ↑

Start   Finish,
First term   The tenth term is
                         the last term

Add 2 to get
the next term
(12 + 2 = 14)

Key Stage 3 Maths Explained - Volume 2 Algebra

If you are asked to start with 50 and then keep adding 5 until you have six **terms** (that is six numbers in the series), the list (or series) would be:

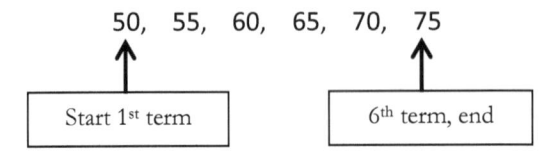

50, 55, 60, 65, 70, 75

↑ Start 1st term   ↑ 6th term, end

You could be asked to start with 2 and **multiply** by 3 until you have 5 terms. This would give you:

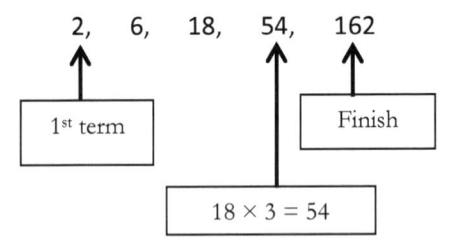

2, 6, 18, 54, 162

↑ 1st term   ↑   ↑ Finish

18 × 3 = 54

Or you might be asked to start with 1215, **divide** by 3 and give 6 terms.
So, you would get:

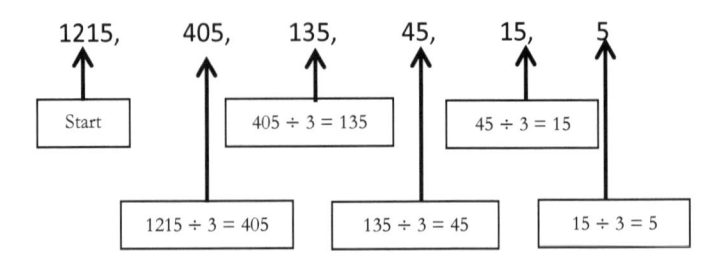

1215, 405, 135, 45, 15, 5

↑ Start   ↑ 405 ÷ 3 = 135   ↑   ↑ 45 ÷ 3 = 15   ↑

1215 ÷ 3 = 405   135 ÷ 3 = 45   15 ÷ 3 = 5

Series are not complicated. They are the patterns which you can use to get from small numbers to large numbers or from large numbers to small numbers. The patterns obey rules which are quite straight forward.

There is no exercise on this chapter.

Chapter 14 – Finding a Term of an Arithmetic Series

Series such as: 2, 4, 6, 8, 10 which were illustrated at the start of the last chapter, are known as "Arithmetic Series". Arithmetic series go from one term to the next by adding or subtracting a number known as the **common difference.** In this case the common difference is 2.

To write down an arithmetic series you need to know:

① The first number, that is the **first term;**

② The number you add to or subtract from each term, that is **the common difference;**

③ Where to stop. Which is **the last term or the number of terms** in the series.

To write down an arithmetic series with the first term 6, the common difference 3, and the last term 33. Start with 6, keep adding 3 until you get to 33 and then stop.

(The number of the term) (1) (2) (3) (4) (5) (6) (7) (8) (9) (10)

(The value of the term) 6 9 12 15 18 21 24 27 30 33

(Common Difference)   +3 +3 +3 +3 +3 +3 +3 +3 +3

Look at the series again. You could have been asked to write a series with the first term 6, the common difference 3, and ten terms. You would get exactly the same series.

Key Stage 3 Maths Explained - Volume 2 Algebra

These are the steps:

1) Write down the first term
2) Add the common difference and write down the next term.
3) Continue doing this until you have reached the correct number of terms or the given last term. Then stop.

There is one more step. You could be asked to find the 20th number in the series. Let's use the same series again. 6, 9, 12, ... Do you really need to write all the terms up to the 20th?

To get the fifth term you write:

(The number of the term)	(1)	(2)	(3)	(4)	(5)
(The value of the term)	6	9	12	15	18
(Common Difference)		+3	+3	+3	+3

This is adding **four** lots of 3. The series starts with a 6 and ends with 18. There are 5 numbers and 4 gaps. So, to get from the 1st to the 5th term you add on **4** lots of 3.

To get from the 1st to the 9th term you add on 8 lots of 3.

(The number of the term)	(1)	(2)	(3)	(4)	(5)	(6)	(7)	(8)	(9)
(The value of the term)	6	9	12	15	18	21	24	27	30
(Common Difference)		+3	+3	+3	+3	+3	+3	+3	+3

So, the 9th term is 6 + (8 × 3) = 6 + 24 = 30
The 5th term is 6 + (4 × 3) = 18.
The formula for the nth term is 6 + (n – 1) × 3.
If the first term is **a** and the common difference is **d**, then the value of nth term is: a + (n – 1) d.

So, the value of the 20th term is
6 + (20 – 1) × 3 = 6 + 3 × 19 = 6 + 58 = 64

Chapter 14 – Finding a Term of an Arithmetic Series

Exercise 14

Write out the series with:

	First term	Common difference	Number of terms
1)	5	2	9
2)	3	5	8
3)	9	3	10
4)	11	4	9
5)	14	6	9
6)	16	5	10

The answers are on the next page

Key Stage 3 Maths Explained - Volume 2 Algebra

Answers to Exercise 14

1) 5, 7, 9, 11, 13, 15, 17, 19, 21

2) 3, 8, 13, 18, 23, 28, 33, 38

3) 9, 12, 15, 18, 21, 24, 27, 30, 33, 36

4) 11, 15, 19, 23, 27, 31, 35, 39, 43

5) 14, 20, 26, 32, 38, 44, 50, 56, 62

6) 16, 21, 26, 31, 36, 41, 46, 51, 56, 61

Chapter 15 - Arithmetic Series, With Negative Differences

Negative Differences

Earlier chapters looked at series of numbers which went from small to large. This chapter deals with series which go from large to small.

Look at this series 28, 24, 20, 16

As before you need to know three things:

1) Which number to start with,
2) How much you **subtract** to go from one number to the next,
3) When to stop. (the number of terms).

This series starts with 28 and you **subtract** 4 each time.

So, if you are asked to find eight numbers in the series they will be:
28, 24, 20, 16, 12, 8, 4, 0
The series goes down in steps of 4.

Suppose you are asked to write the first 6 terms of a series which starts with 50 and has a common difference of —5. You would write:

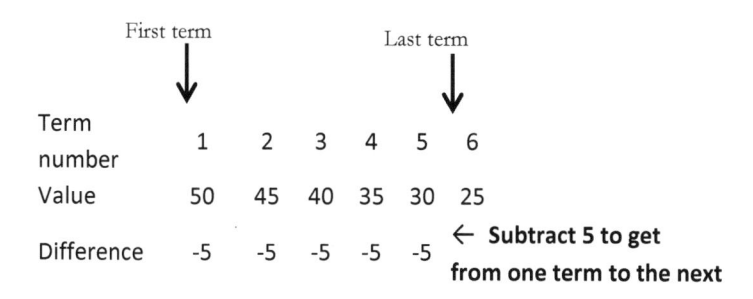

	First term				Last term	
Term number	1	2	3	4	5	6
Value	50	45	40	35	30	25
Difference	-5	-5	-5	-5	-5	← Subtract 5 to get from one term to the next

Key Stage 3 Maths Explained - Volume 2 Algebra

If you are told that the first term is 80, the common difference is -5 and you are asked to find the 10th term, you must get the next 9 values. You can use a **similar** formula to the one in the last chapter.

First plus 9 more gives 10 terms.

The first term is 80 and you are asked to find the 10th term so you must take away **nine** lots of 5 and the tenth term will be 80 – (9 × 5)

which is the same as 80 + (9 × –5)

$$80 - (9 \times 5) = 80 - 45$$
$$= 35$$

The series is: 80, 75, 70, 65, 60, 55, 50, 45, 40, 35

So, if you get a series which gets smaller then you just keep taking away instead of adding.

The formula which gives you the nth term becomes $a - (n - 1)d$
Where **a** is the first term **d** is the difference between terms (the **common difference**) and n is the number of terms.

The two formulae for the nth term are:
$a + (n - 1)d$ if the series is getting larger as you go on,
$a - (n - 1)d$ if the series is getting smaller as you go on.

Chapter 15 - Arithmetic Series, With Negative Differences

Exercise 15

Write out the following series in full:

	First term	Common difference	Number of terms
1)	45	−5	8
2)	64	−8	8
3)	60	−6	9
4)	27	−3	8
5)	54	−7	8
6)	99	−12	6

The answers are on the next page

Key Stage 3 Maths Explained - Volume 2 Algebra

Answers to exercise 15

1) 45, 40, 35, 30, 25, 20, 15, 10

2) 64, 56, 48, 42, 40, 32, 24, 16

3) 60, 54, 48, 42, 36, 30, 24, 18, 12

4) 27, 24, 21, 18, 15, 12, 9, 6

5) 54, 47, 40, 33, 26, 20, 13, 6

6) 99 87, 75, 63, 51, 39

Chapter 16 – Finding the nth Term in a Series

If you are told that a series starts with 5 and that the **common difference** between the terms is 4,
then the series will be 5, 9, 13, 17, 21, 25, 29, 33, 37 … and on and on…. So the nth term will be a + (n – 1) d

If **a** (the first term) is 5,
and **d** (the difference between terms) is 4,
and **n** is 20.

Then the 20th term is   5 + (20 – 1) × 4
= 5 + 19 × 4
= 5 + 76
= 81

To check (but don't do this on all examples)

Term number	1	2	3	4	5	6	7	8	9	10	11	12	13	14	15	16	17	18	19	20
Value	5	9	13	17	21	25	29	33	37	41	45	49	53	57	61	65	69	73	77	81
Difference Between values		+4	+4	+4	+4	+4	+4	+4	+4	+4	+4	+4	+4	+4	+4	+4	+4	+4	+4	+4

You have added 19 lots of 4 = 19 × 4 = 76
You have added these to 5, so the 20th number is 76 + 5 = 81

With the formula: Value of nth term = a + (n -1)d
you can find the value of any term; the 31st, 89th or the 415th if you need to, without writing out the series.

If you are asked to find the 31st term of this series you use the formula:

31st term = a + (31 – 1)d
= 5 + 30 × 4
= 5 + 120 = 125
The value of the 31st term is 125.

Key Stage 3 Maths Explained - Volume 2 Algebra

This formula works just as well if the difference is a negative number.

If you are told that a series starts at 17 and has a common difference of -3 you could write 17, 14, 11, …. and so on,

And if you were also asked to find the 21st term of this series the formula would tell you that it is:

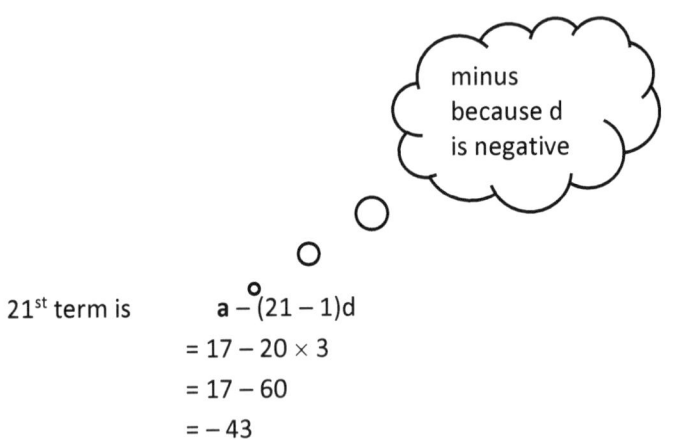

minus because d is negative

21st term is $a - (21 - 1)d$
= 17 − 20 × 3
= 17 − 60
= − 43

So, if you were asked to find the 37th term as well you would write the formula:

37st term is $a - (37 - 1)d$
= 17 − 36 × 3
= 17 − 108
= − 91

The 37th term is − 91

Chapter 16 – Finding the nth Term in a Series

Try this on the numbers in exercise 16.

Exercise 16

Take a as the starting number, d as the common difference and find the two terms with the numbers given in column n.

	a	d	n		a	d	n
1)	9	3	8th and 21st	4)	10	-5	11th and 31st
2)	8	-4	6th and 37th	5)	14	6	7th and 55th
3)	4	6	9th and 29th	6)	16	5	8th and 73th

The answers are on the next page

Key Stage 3 Maths Explained - Volume 2 Algebra

Answers to Exercise 16

1) The 8th term is $9 + (8 - 1)3 = 30$

    The 21st term is $9 + (21 - 1)3 = 69$

2) The 6th term is $8 - (6 - 1)4 = -12$

    The 21st term is $8 - (21 - 1)4 = -72$

3) The 9th term is $4 + (9 - 1)6 = 52$

    The 29st term is $4 + (29 - 1)6 = 172$

4) The 11th term is $10 - (11 - 1)5 = -40$

    The 31st term is $10 - (31 - 1)5 = -140$

5) The 7th term is $14 + (7 - 1)6 = 50$

    The 55th term is $14 + (55 - 1)6 = 338$

6) The 8th term is $16 + (8 - 1)5 = 51$

    The 73th term is $16 + (73 - 1)5 = 376$

Chapter 17 – Geometric Series

Geometric series are different. Instead of adding or subtracting a number to go from one term to the next, in a geometric series we have to **multiply** one term by a number to get the next term in the series.

For example: 1, 2, 4, 8, 16, 32 is a geometric series.
This could be written as:
1, 1 × 2, 1 × 2 × 2, 1 × 2 × 2 × 2, 1 × 2 × 2 × 2 × 2 and so on for as long as you like.
It is of course simpler to write: 1, 2, 4, 8, 16, 32.
In this series the starting number is 1, the multiplier is 2 and we have written 6 terms.

Geometric series, with a multiplier bigger than 1, can quickly get very large. In the series 1, 2, 4, … the 8th term is 128, the 10th is 512 and the 12th term is 2048.

Here is another geometric series. This one starts at 8 and has a multiplier 1·2 The first five terms are:

8, 8 × 1·2, 8 × 1·2 × 1·2, 8 × 1·2 × 1·2 × 1·2, 8 × 1·2 × 1·2 × 1·2× 1·2

Or to save writing rows of × 1·2 you could use the powers notation and write:

8, 8 × 1·2, 8 × 1·2^2, 8 × 1·2^3, 8 × 1·2^4

If you multiply out the terms (use your calculator} in this series, you will get the series as:

8,   9·6,   11·25,   13.825,   16·5888

The easiest way to get the next term in this series is to multiply the last term you have found by 1·2.

So, to get from the 1st to the 5th term you multiply each term by 1·2.

(The number of the term)	(1)	(2)	(3)	(4)	(5)
(The value of the term)	8	9·6,	11·25,	13.825,	16·5888
(Multiplier)		×1·2	×1·2	×1·2	×1·2

In chapter16 we found that the value of nth term of an arithmetic series is **a + (n – 1) d**.

You can do the same thing for a geometric series.

If the starting number in a series is **a**, and the multiplier which takes us from one term to the next is **m**, then the value of the **n**th term is **a × m**$^{(n-1)}$.

So if you are asked to find the first three terms in the series which starts with 8, and has a multiplier of 1·2 you will get the series 8, 9·6, 11·25, which we have already found. If you are then asked to find the tenth term there is no need to work them all out. You just use the formula **a × m**$^{(n-1)}$ and write:

The tenth term is $8 × 1·2^{10-1} = 8 × 1·2^9$
$= 8 × 5·159780352$
$= 41·278242816$

or 41·278 to three decimal places.

Geometric series with multipliers smaller than 1 have terms which get smaller the further you go on. If we start with 1 and a multiplier of 0·5 we will get a series with terms: 1, 0·5, 0·25, 0·125, 0·0625, 0·03125, …. it will eventually get very very small.

Chapter 17 – Geometric Series

Exercise 17

Find the first six terms and the 10th and 20th terms of the following series: (use your calculator and give three significant figures after the decimal point.)

Do remember that the number you started with is the first number, so you need to find another five terms to make a total of six

A tip from your Tutor

1) Start at 9 and use a multiplier of 2

2) Start at 10 and use a multiplier of 1·1

3) Start at 1 and use 0·9 as a multiplier

4) Start at 5 and use a multiplier of 0·5

The answers are on the next page

Key Stage 3 Maths Explained - Volume 2 Algebra

Answers to Exercise 17

1) The first six terms of the geometric series which starts at 9 and has a multiplier of 2 are: 9, 18, 36, 72, 144, 288

The tenth term is $9 \times 2^{(10-1)} = 9 \times 2^9 = 9 \times 512 = 4608$
The 20th term is $9 \times 2^{(20-1)} = 9 \times 2^{19} = 9 \times 524288 = 4718592$

2) The first six terms of the geometric series which starts at 10 and has a multiplier of 1·1 are: 10, 11, 12·1, 13·31, 14·641, 16·105

The tenth term is $10 \times 1 \cdot 1^{(10-1)} = 10 \times 1 \cdot 1^9 = 10 \times 2 \cdot 35794$
$= 23 \cdot 578$ to 3 decimal places
The 20th term is $10 \times 1 \cdot 1^{(20-1)} = 10 \times 1 \cdot 1^{19} = 10 \times 6 \cdot 11591$
$= 61 \cdot 159$ to 3 decimal places.

3) The first six terms of the geometric series which starts at 1 and use 0·9 as a multiplier are: 1, 0·9, 0·81, 0·729, 0·6561, 0·590(49)

The tenth term is $1 \times 0 \cdot 9^{(10-1)} = 1 \times 0 \cdot 9^9 = 1 \times 0 \cdot 387420$
$= 0.387$ to 3 decimal places
The 20th term is $1 \times 0 \cdot 9^{(20-1)} = 1 \times 0 \cdot 9^{19} = 1 \times 0 \cdot 135085$
$= 0 \cdot 135$ to 3 decimal places.

4) The first six terms of the geometric series which starts at 5 and use 0·5 as a multiplier are: 5, 2·5, 1·25, 0·6253, 0·3125, 0·015625

The tenth term is $5 \times 0 \cdot 5^{(10-1)} = 5 \times 0 \cdot 5^9 = 5 \times 0.0019531$
$= 0 \cdot 00977$ to 3 significant figures
The 20th term is $5 \times 0 \cdot 5^{(20-1)} = 5 \times 0 \cdot 5^{19} = 5 \times 0 \cdot 0000019074$
$= 0 \cdot 00000954$ to 3 significant figures.

Chapter 18 – Fibonacci and Other Series

Fibonacci series

Another important series can be made in the following way.

Start with 1,
then another 1. Add them together, making 2.
So, the first three terms are: 1, 1, 2.

Now add the 2 to the previous number, making 3.
Then add the three to the previous number, which is 2, making 5.

The series is now 1, 1, 2, 3, 5,
Continue adding the last two terms in the series to get the next.

1, 1, 2, 3, 5, 8, 13, 21, 34, 55, 89, 144, 233, 377, 610……

This series was invented by an Italian mathematician called "Fibonacci". It has two interesting features.

First, if you divide any two numbers in the series by the number just before it you get a number close to 1.618…

Try it! Use your calculator.
$$\frac{21}{13} = 1.615...$$

$$\frac{233}{144} = 1.61805...$$

$$\frac{610}{377} = 1.618037...$$

Key Stage 3 Maths Explained - Volume 2 Algebra

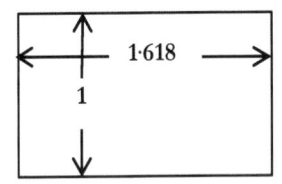

A rectangle with this ratio of width to height is considered to be the easiest shape to look at. Television screens are made in this shape.

Many paintings of landscapes and many classical buildings have this same ratio of width to height. Here is a drawing of a classical temple. It was traced from a photograph

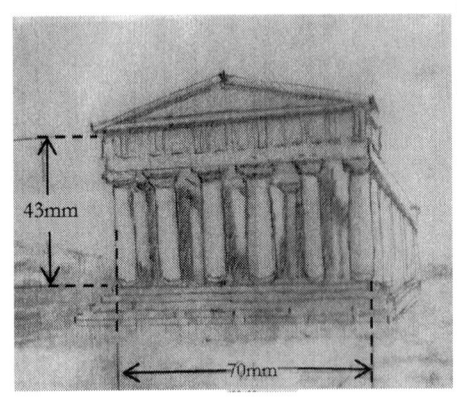

On the photograph the width of the temple was 70 mm and its height from the pavement to the point shown was 43 mm.

The ratio $\frac{70}{43} = 1.63$, is not far from the Fibonacci ratio of 1.618

Chapter 18 – Fibonacci and Other Series

Second,

Many things in the natural world can be found with numbers from the Fibonacci series. If you find a flower with thirteen petals in its inner ring, it is likely to have 21 petals in the next ring, like this marigold.

Again, many curled sea shells, where you can count growth cells, will have numbers of cells in each ring which come from the Fibonacci series.

Other Series

Later on, you will come across a number of other series which let us calculate useful numbers like π, and the sine and cosine of an angle.

Exercise 18

1) The 14th term of the Fibonacci series is 377. The 15th term is 610. Work out the next four terms.

2) Calculate the ratio of each larger to the smaller term to four decimal places.

The answers are on the next page

Key Stage 3 Maths Explained - Volume 2 Algebra

Answers to Exercise 18

1) The sixteenth term is 377 + 610 = 987

   The seventeenth term is 610 + 987 = 1597

   The eighteenth term is 987 + 1597 = 2584

   The nineteenth term is 1598 + 2584 = 4182

2) To four significant figures, the ratios are:

   987 ÷ 610 = 1.6180 (3)

   1597 ÷ 987 = 1.6190 (4)

   2584 ÷ 1597 = 1.6180 (3)

   4182 ÷ 2584 = 1.6184 (2)

Entire Part 2n

Rearranging and Solving Equations

Here is a linear equation: $3x + 2 = 2x - 3$.
What is the value of x?
The terms in x, the $3x$ and the $2x$, need to be on the left-hand side of the equals sign. So, the first step is to move the $2x$ to join the $3x$.

(Here we are using the word **term** to mean any item in an equation made up of a number and a variable, such as '$3x$' which have been multiplied together)

The rule in rearranging equations is that you must always do the same thing to both side of the equation, or it won't balance

Two things to remember

You need to get both the terms in x on the left-hand side of the equation. You can do this by subtracting $2x$ from both sides.

$3x - 2x + 2 = 2x - 2x - 3$

Or $x + 2 = -3$. Now we can get all the numbers onto the right-hand side of the equals sign by subtracting 2 from both sides.

$x + 2 - 2 = -3 - 2$ so $x = -5$

Another way to look at this is to say that when you move any piece of the equation across the equals sign you change its sign from + to − or − to +.

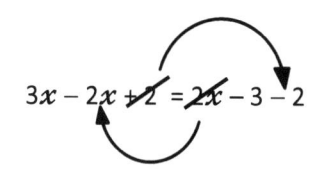

$3x - 2x + 2 = 2x - 3 - 2$

Key Stage 3 Maths Explained - Volume 2 Algebra

To sum up:

Rule 1: Rearrange the terms. While doing this keep the terms in one piece. The $2x$ moves as $2x$.

Remember

Rule 2: A plus sign crossing the equals sign becomes a minus, and a minus sign crossing the equals sign becomes a plus.

Suppose we have this equation: $\quad 4x = 20$.

$4x$ means 4 times x, so the equation is really $4 \times x = 20$
Whatever we do to one side of an equation we must do to the other, or the equation will cease to be an equality!

To produce an $x =$ equation we will have to divide both sides by 4
This gives $\dfrac{4x}{4} = \dfrac{20}{4}$ or $x = 5$

Another way of looking at this is to say that as the 4 moves across the equals sign it turns from a multiply to a divide, or the 4 on top turns to 4 underneath.

$$4x = \dfrac{20}{4} \quad \text{or} \quad x = 5$$

We could have a different equation which says, $\dfrac{x}{3} = 4$, in which case multiply both sides by 3, which would give $x = 4 \times 3 = 12$. In this case the divide goes to multiply when it crosses the equals sign. Either way the underneath figure on one side, goes to the top on the other side of the = sign.

Entire Part 2n

So, we have two more rules:

Rule 3: Multiply goes to divide or top goes to bottom on crossing the equals sign, and

Remember

Rule 4: Divide goes to multiply or bottom goes to top on crossing the equals sign.

Here is another equation: $6x - 5 = 3x + 4$.

The first step is to rearrange the terms. The $6x$ is on the correct side of the equals sign, so it stays put. The $3x$ is on the other side. As it has no sign written in front of it, we can assume that it is $+3x$. When it moves to the left-hand side it becomes $-3x$.

$$6x - 3x - 5 = +4$$

The number 4 is on the correct side, so it can stay where it is. The -5 is on the wrong side so it crosses the equals sign and becomes $+5$.

$$6x - 3x = +4 + 5$$

Now that all the terms are correctly positioned we can combine them.

$6x - 3x = 3x$, and $4 + 5 = 9$ which gives the equation as $3x = 9$.

What we do to one side of the equation we must do to the other.
So, divide both sides by 3 to give $\dfrac{3x}{3} = \dfrac{9}{3}$ or $x = 3$.

Another way of looking at this is to say that as the 3 moves across the equals sign it turns from a multiply to a divide, or the 3 on top turns to 3 underneath. $x\cancel{3} = \dfrac{9}{3}$

Whichever way you remember it the answer is $x = 3$

Key Stage 3 Maths Explained - Volume 2 Algebra

Here is another equation.

$6x - 1 = 4x + 7$

Step 1 is to rearrange the equation.
The $6x$ and the 7 stay put. The -1 crosses the equals and becomes $+1$, and the $4x$ crosses onto the left side and becomes $-4x$.

$6x - 4x = +7 + 1$

Step 2 is to simplify this by adding and subtracting.
$6x - 4x = 2x$ and $7 + 1 = 8$ so the equation becomes $2x = 8$
Now the 2 crosses the = and becomes divide by 2, giving 4.
So $x = 4$

Here is a slightly more complicated **expression,** but the steps are just the same.

(The term **expression** is used for any short piece of algebra)

$$\frac{x}{2} + 3 = \frac{x}{4} + 8$$

The $\frac{x}{2}$ and the $+8$ are on their correct sides so they don't move.
The $+3$ goes over to the right-hand side of the equals becoming -3 as it goes. The $\frac{x}{4}$ also crosses, becoming $-\frac{x}{4}$.

So, the equation now looks like this: $\frac{x}{2} - \frac{x}{4} = +8 - 3$

$$\frac{x}{2} \times \frac{2}{2} - \frac{x}{4} = +8 - 3$$

so $\frac{2x}{4} - \frac{x}{4} = 5$

or $x = 5 \times 4 = 20$

Entire Part 2n

Next, simplify $4(x + 2) = 2(x + 10)$

This looks even worse; but it only involves one more step.
First **multiply out the brackets**.
4 times $x = 4x$
4 times $2 = 8$
2 times $x = 2x$
2 times $10 = 20$

This gives $4x + 8 = 2x + 20$

Now this is the type of equation you are used to. So, rearrange the terms. The $4x$ and the 20 stay put. The +8 crosses the equals sign and becomes –8, and the $2x$ crosses the equals sign and becomes – $2x$.
The equation is now $4x - 2x = + 20 - 8 = 12$
Combining the terms gives $2x = 12$
Taking the 2 across gives $x = \dfrac{12}{2} = 6$, so **$x = 6$**.

Changing the subject of an equation

In chapter 10 we examined the equation of a straight line. It looked like this:

$$y = mx + c$$

When plotted on the x, axis this gives a straight line which crosses the y axis at 'c' and has a slope or gradient of 'm'.
x can be called **the subject** of the equation.

If we are given several values of x we can put them into the equation and find the values of y which go with each value of x.

Now what if was the other way around? We are given some values of y and asked to find the value of x which goes with each one of them

Key Stage 3 Maths Explained - Volume 2 Algebra

Turn the equation round to make y the subject. This is known as **changing the subject** of the equation.

We started with $\qquad y = mx + c$
Move mx to the left-hand side of the equation and change its sign.
This gives $\qquad y - mx = c$

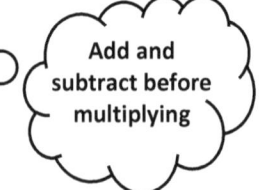

Add and subtract before multiplying

Now move y to the left-hand side and change its sign
$$- mx = c - y$$

Change **all** the signs on both sides, so that $\quad mx = -c + y$
and divide both sides by m

The equation is now $\qquad x = \dfrac{1}{m}(y - c)$

$\qquad\qquad\qquad$ or $\quad x = \dfrac{1}{m}y - \dfrac{c}{m}$

We have changed the subject of the equation from x to y

Here is another example, a little more complicated:

$y + 7x = 5x + 3y + 6 \qquad$ Make x the subject of the equation.

Step 1 Move the $5x$ to the left-hand side and change its sign as it crosses the =
$$y + 7 - 5x = 3y + 6$$

Step 2 Move the y to the right-hand side and change its sign as it goes.
$$7 - 5x = 3y - y + 6$$
Collect terms: $\qquad\qquad\quad 2x = 2y + 6$
Divide both sides by 2 $\qquad x = y + 3$
This is now an equation to give the values of x

Entire Part 2n

Exercise 19. Find the value of x

1. $4x - 2 = 2x + 4$

2. $6x - 3 = 3x + 6$

3. $3x - 2 = 2x + 4$

4. $7x + 11 = 2x + 1$

5. $9x = 27$

6. $5x = -20$

7. $2x - 8 = 5x + 4.$

8. $6x - 8 = 3x + 4.$

9. $3x + 6 = 8x - 9.$

10. $\dfrac{x}{3} + 5 = \dfrac{x}{9} - 7$

11. $\dfrac{x}{4} - 3 = \dfrac{x}{12} - 5$

12. $\dfrac{x}{9} - 5 = \dfrac{x}{3} - 7$

13. $4(x - 3) = 3(x - 4)$

14. $3(x + 3) = 5(x + 1)$

15. $3(x + 4) = 5(x - 2)$

16. $4(x + 2) = 7(x + 1) - 14$

17. $3(x - 2) + 9 = 5(x - 1)$

18. $5(x + 3) - 3 = 6(x - 1) - 2$

In questions 19 to 24 change the subject of the equation from y to x.

19. $y = 5x + 3$

20. $3y = 12x + 9$

21. $-2y = 3y - 5x - 10$

22. $3y = x - 6y + 9$

23. $2y + x = 8y - 5x + 12$

24. $3y = 3x - 9y - 12$

The answers are on the next page

Key Stage 3 Maths Explained - Volume 2 Algebra

Answers to Exercise 19

1. $x = 3$
2. $x = 3$
3. $x = 6$
4. $x = -2$
5. $x = 3$
6. $x = -4$
7. $x = -4$
8. $x = 4$
9. $x = 3$
10. $x = -54$
11. $x = -12$
12. $x = 9$
13. $x = 0$
14. $x = 2$
15. $x = 3$
16. $x = 5$
17. $x = 4$
18. $x = 20$
19. $x = \frac{1}{5}y - \frac{3}{5}$
20. $x = \frac{1}{4}y - \frac{3}{4}$
21. $x = y + 2$
22. $x = 9y - 9$
23. $x = y + 2$
24. $x = 4y + 4$

Chapter 20 – Simultaneous Equations, Introduction

Simultaneous Equations sound odd, but they are quite simple. You are given two equations. They both contain x and y.
You are not told the value of either x or y.

For example:

$$x + y = 10 \quad \text{———— equation ①}$$
$$x - y = 2. \quad \text{———— equation ②}$$

Write them down under each other
You can add these equations together but **do write down what you are doing!**

Add equation ② to equation ①

$$x + y = 10$$
$$x - y = 2. \; +$$
$$2x \;\; = 12$$

So $x = \dfrac{2x}{2} = \dfrac{12}{2} = 6$

Put $x = 6$ into equation ②
$$6 - y = 2.$$
$$\text{So, } 6 - 2 = y$$

> The rule is change sides and change signs

Therefore $y = 4$
You have solved both equations and found that $x = 6$ and $y = 4$

Check your answer by putting both solutions into equation ①
(use ① because you have already used ①)

6 + 4 = 10, correct.

Key Stage 3 Maths Explained - Volume 2 Algebra

Here is another example:

If $x + y = 15$ and $x - y = 1$ find the values of x and y

	$x + y = 15$	——— ①
	$x - y = 1$	——— ②
Add ① to ②	$2x + 0 = 16$	——— ③
So	$2x = 16$	——— ④
Divide both sides by 2	$x = 8$	——— ⑤

Put 8 for x in ① $8 + y = 15$

Take the 8 to the other side $y = 15 - 8$

So $y = 7$

The answer is $x = 8$, $=7$

Check by putting $= 8$, and $y = 7$

into equation ②. $(x - y = 1)$

$8 - 7 = 1$ correct!

Chapter 21 – Simultaneous Equations with the same sign

The simultaneous equations in the last chapter had one equation with a plus sign and one with a minus sign. Now here are some with two plus signs and some extra numbers. Don't worry they are not difficult.

$$3x + y = 26 \quad \text{———} \quad ①$$
$$2x + y = 18 \quad \text{———} \quad ②$$

Subtract ② from ① and you get $\quad x = 8 \quad$ ——— ③

Put $x = 8$ into equation ① $\quad 3 \times 8 + y = 26 \quad$ ——— ④

$$24 + y = 26 \quad \text{———} \quad ⑤$$

Take the 24 to the other side

The rule is change sides and change signs

$+ 24 + y = 26$

$y = 26 - 24$

$y = 2$

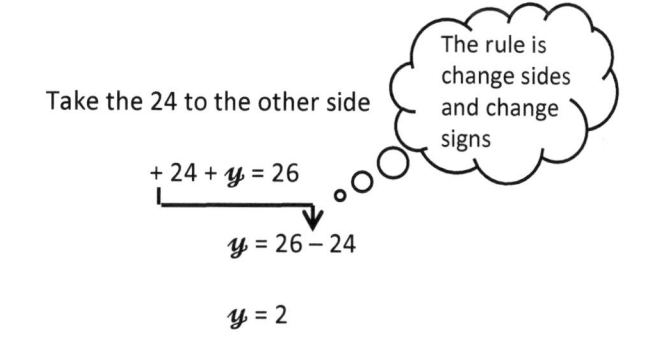

The answer is $x = 8$ and $y = 2$

Check by putting $x = 8$, $y = 2$ into equation ②.

$2x + y = 18$, gives $2 \times 8 + 2 = 18 \qquad$ which is correct.

Key Stage 3 Maths Explained - Volume 2 Algebra

Here is another example:

$$5x - y = 30 \quad \text{————} \quad ①$$
$$2x - y = 6 \quad \text{————} \quad ②$$

To find the value of x, subtract equation ② from equation ①.

$$5x - y = 30 \quad \text{————} \quad ①$$
$$2x - y = 6 \quad \text{————} \quad ②$$

$5x - 2x = 3x$, $-y - (-y) = 0$ and $30 - 6 = 24$.

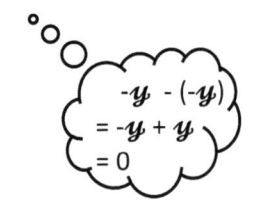

(thought bubble: $-y - (-y) = -y + y = 0$)

So $3x = 24$ and $x = \dfrac{24}{3} = 8$.

Now substitute 8 for x in equation ②.

$2 \times 8 - y = 6$, which gives $16 - y = 6$

$-y = 6 - 16 = -10$

Now change signs on both sides

So $y = 10$

The answer is $x = 8$ and $y = 10$

To check your answer put these numbers into equation ①,

$$5 \times 8 - 10 = 40 - 10 = 30$$

So, we have the correct answer.

Chapter 22 – Simultaneous Equations with Different Constants

What do you do if there are different constants in the equations? Suppose you have a pair of equations like this:

$3x - 2y = 1$ —————— ①
$5x + 4y = 53$ —————— ②

Merely adding or subtracting the two equations won't work!

So, what do you do? You can always multiply both sides of an equation by any number without changing the equation, providing you always **multiply both sides by the same number.**

Multiply all the numbers in equation ① by 2, and you get a new equation ③.

$$6x - 4y = 2 \quad —————— ③$$

Now write equation ② $\quad 5x + 4y = 53 \quad —————— ②$

Now you can add ③ to ②
and get: $6x + 5x - 4y + 4y = 2 + 53 = 55$

So $11x = 55$,

$$x = \frac{55}{11} = 5$$

So $x = 5$

Substitute $x = 5$ in equation ② and you get

$5 \times 5 + 4y = 53$ —————— ④

So, $25 + 4y = 53$

or $4y = 53 - 25 = 28 \quad y = \frac{28}{4} = 7$

Key Stage 3 Maths Explained - Volume 2 Algebra

To check, substitute for x and y in equation ①.

$3 \times 5 - 2 \times 7 = 15 - 14 = 1$. Your answer is correct.

$$x = 5, y = 7$$

Now let's try one more of these:

$3x - 7y = 36$ ——— ①
$9x - 5y = 60$ ——— ②

If you multiply both sides of equation ① by 3 (which doesn't change the equation)
You get:

$9x - 21y = 108$ ——— ③
$9x - 5y = 60$ ——— ②

Subtract equation ② from ③ and you get:

$-16y = 48$ so $y = \dfrac{48}{-16} = -3$

Now put -3 for y into equation ②
(but you could use either ① or ②)

and you get $9x - 5 \times (-3) = 60$, which becomes $9x + 15 = 60$

Which gives you $9x = 45$

$$x = \dfrac{45}{9} = 5$$

So, the answer is $x = 5$ and $y = -3$

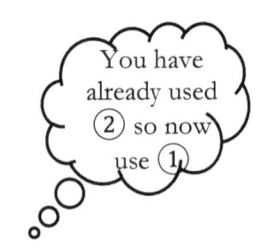

You have already used ② so now use ①

Once again check by putting $x = 5$, $y = -3$ into ①, $3x - 7y = 36$,

So, $3 \times 5 - 7 \times (-3) = 15 + 21 = 36$, which is correct.

Chapter 22 – Simultaneous Equations with Different Constants

What do you do if there is no simple way of changing the equations so that there is the same number (or **coefficient**) in front of either x or y?

Look at this pair of equations:

$3x - 2y = -1$ ———— ①
$5x + 7y = 50$ ———— ②

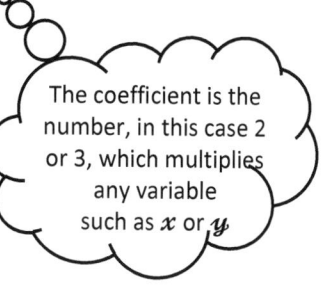

> The coefficient is the number, in this case 2 or 3, which multiplies any variable such as x or y

Here's how you can make the number in front of both x's the same. Multiply both sides of equation ① by 5
(the coefficient of x in equation ②)
and multiply both sides of equation ② by 3
(the coefficient of x in equation ①)

This gives you two new equations ③ and ④.

$5 \times 3x - 5 \times 2y = -1 \times 5$ ———— ③
$3 \times 5x + 3 \times 7y = 3 \times 50$ ———— ④

When you have multiplied you get

$15x - 10y = -5$ ———— ③
$15x + 21y = 150$ ———— ④

Now subtract both sides of equation ③ from equation ④ to give equation ⑤.

$15x - 15x + 21y - (-10)y = 150 - (-5)$ ———— ⑤

$31y = 155,$

so $y = \dfrac{155}{31} = 5$

Now put $y = 5$ into equation ④ $15x + 21 \times 5 = 150$,

This gives $15x = 150 - 105$, so $x = \dfrac{45}{15} = 3$

The answer is $x = 3$
and $y = 5$
Once again check your answer by putting $x = 3$ and $y = 5$ into equation ①
This gives us $3 \times 3 - 2 \times 5 = 9 - 10 = -1$, so the answer is correct.

Here is a pair of simultaneous equations

$ax + by = d$ ——— ①
$ex - fy = g$ ——— ②

Here a, b, d, e, f and g stand for numbers which, at the moment we don't know.

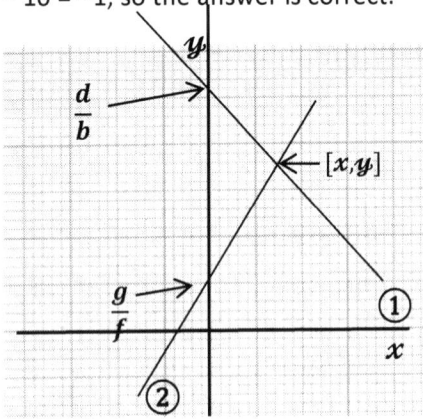

Figure 1

This is the way we usually write these equations. Both are actually the equations of straight lines see figure 1. We can see this if we re-arrange the equations putting y on the left-hand side.

When we do this equation ① becomes: $by = d - ax$
and equation ② becomes: $-fy = g - ex$

Dividing both sides of ① by b and both sides of ② by f creates two equations in the familiar form of the equations of straight lines:

$y = -\dfrac{a}{b}x + \dfrac{d}{b}$ ——— ①

and $y = +\dfrac{e}{f}x + \dfrac{g}{f}$ ——— ②

Chapter 22 – Simultaneous Equations with Different Constants

As you will see ① is the equation of a straight line with a slope of $-\frac{a}{b}$ which crosses the x axis at $\frac{d}{b}$, and ② is the equation of a straight line with a slope of $+\frac{e}{f}$ which crosses the x axis at $\frac{g}{f}$. The point at which the two lines cross is [x,y], which is the simultaneous solution to both equations.

Exercise 20 to 22

Find the values of x and y which solve the following pairs of simultaneous equations:

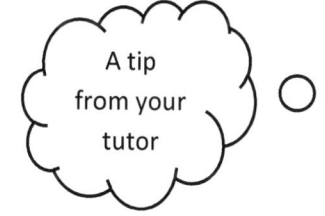

A tip from your tutor: You can find either x or y first. Look for the one which makes the multiplications simpler.

1) $3x + 7y = 29$
   $3x + 3y = 21$

2) $-8x + 6y = 10$
   $+2x + 6y = 20$

3) $3x + 2y = 9$
   $-15x + 5y = -90$

4) $9x + 3y = 12$
   $3x - 7y = 44$

5) $5x - 6y = 3$
   $3x + 5y = 19$

6) $5x + 2y = 25$
   $7x + 5y = 46$

7) $10x + 5y = 40$
   $x + 2y = -5$

8) $-5x + 3y = -22$
   $-7x - 8y = -42$

9) $3x + 5y = 29$
   $7x + 9y = 49$

10) $5x - 11y = 17$
    $-11x + 2y = 118$

The answers and hints are on the next page

Key Stage 3 Maths Explained - Volume 2 Algebra

Hints

In question 3, multiply the first equation by 5.

In question 4, multiply the second equation by 3.

In question 5, multiply the first equation by 6 and the second by 7.

Answers for Exercise 20 to 22

1) $x = 5$, $y = 2$

2) $x = 1$, $y = 3$

3) $x = 5$, $y = -3$

4) $x = 3$, $y = -5$

5) $x = 3$, $y = 2$

6) $x = 3$, $y = 5$

7) $x = 7$, $y = -6$

8) $x = 5$, $y = 1$

9) $x = -2$, $y = 7$

10) $x = -12$, $y = -7$

Chapter 23 – Graphs of Quadratic Equations

In Chapter 6 and Chapter 9 we looked at linear equations where $y = mx + c$. A linear equation can be used to draw the graph of a straight line like the one in figure 1, which has the equation:

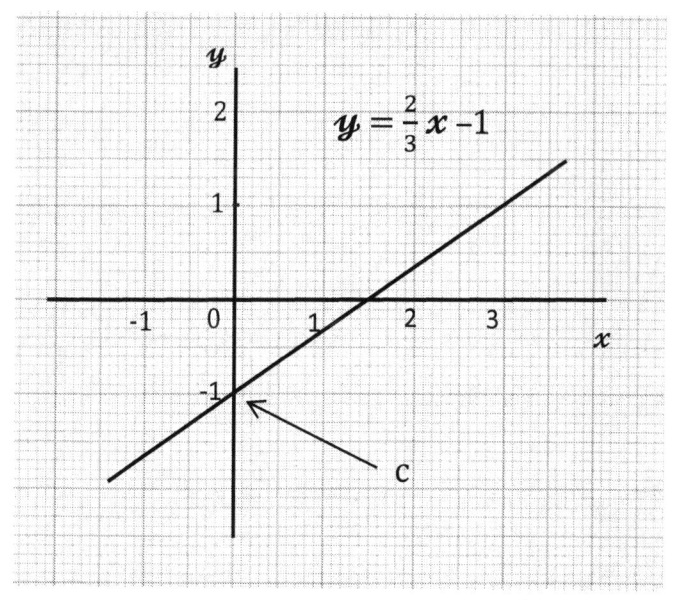

$$y = \frac{2}{3}x - 1$$

Figure 1

When $x = 0$ the line crossed the vertical y axis at the point c. Which is $y = -1$.

The slope or gradient of the line is called **m**.
In this case m = $\frac{2}{3}$, so the y value increases by 2 for every time x increased by 3

Key Stage 3 Maths Explained - Volume 2 Algebra

The simplest **quadratic equation** is $y = x^2$.

Its graph is shown in figure 2. When $x = 0$, then $y = 0$.
When $x = 1$, $y = 1$, as $1 \times 1 = 1$. When $x = 2$, $y = 4$, as $2 \times 2 = 4$.

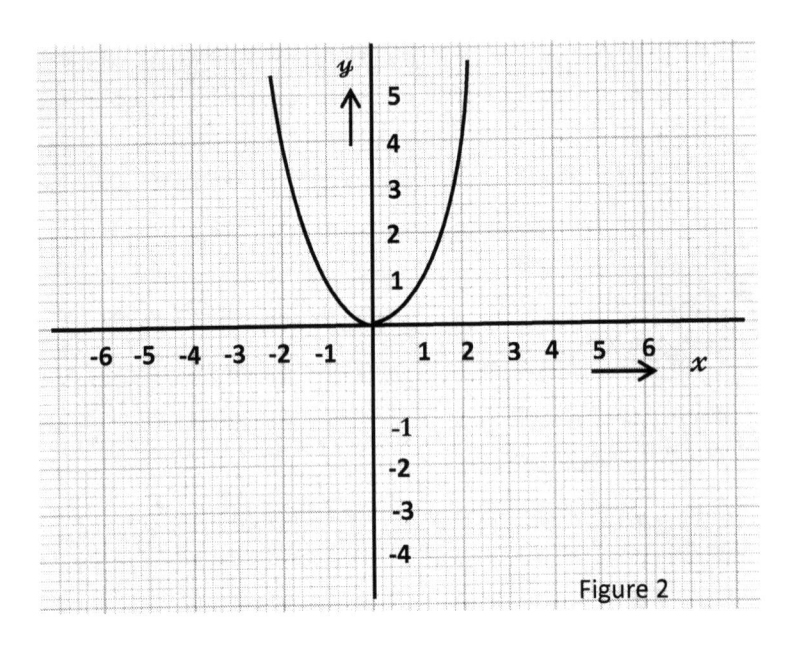

Figure 2

The curve looks the same both sides of the y axis because x^2 is always positive. If $x = -2$, x^2 is still $= 4$ (not -4) because minus times minus is plus. ($-2 \times -2 = 4$).

Chapter 23 – Graphs of Quadratic Equations

$y = ax^2$ is a slightly more complicated quadratic equation. When **a** is 1 you get the graph shown in figure 2. When **a** is less than one y grows more slowly than before and you get a wider curve, see figure3.

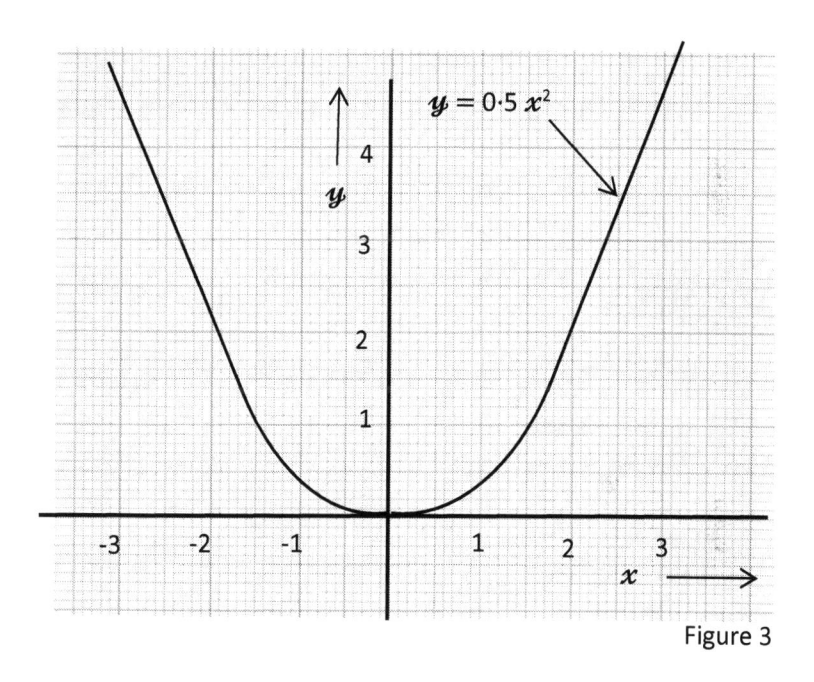

Figure 3

For $y = 0.5\, x^2$ y is still = 0 when $x = 0$, but when $x = 2$ $y = 0.5 \times 2 \times 2 = 2$, and when $x = 3$ $y = 0.5 \times 3 \times 3 = 4.5$

The curve is still the same for both positive and negative values of x because x^2 is always positive.

Now if you make **a**, the coefficient of x, some number greater than 1, the curve gets narrower because y grows more quickly as x gets larger.

$y = 1{\cdot}2\, x^2$

Figure 4

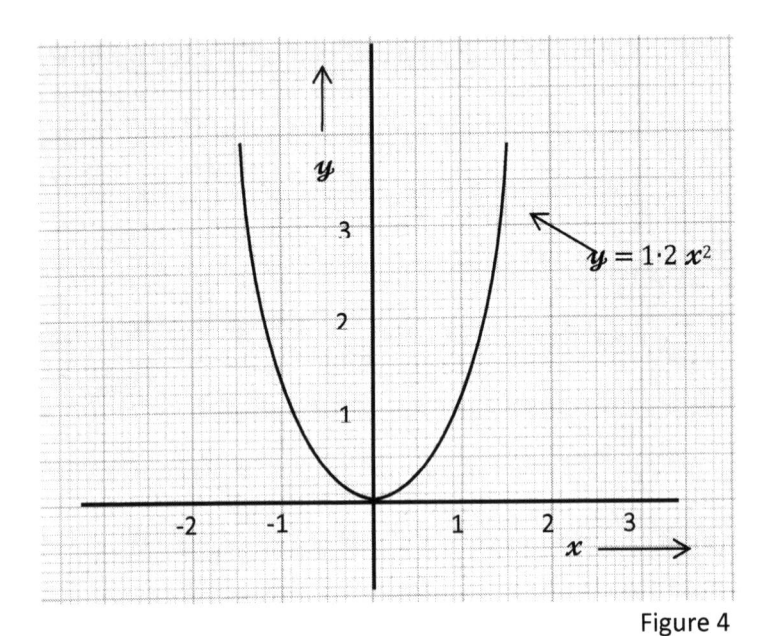

Figure 4 shows a curve for **a** = 1.2

Chapter 23 – Graphs of Quadratic Equations

If we add a constant to the quadratic equation and make it $y = ax^2 + c$, we move the curve up or down the y axis as shown in figure 5

For the lower curve c = - 2. Now, when $y = 0$, $x^2 - 2 = 0$

So, taking the 2 across to the other side of the equation and changing the sign, $x^2 = 2$.

This means that when $y = 0$, $x = \sqrt{2}$ or $x = -\sqrt{2}$.

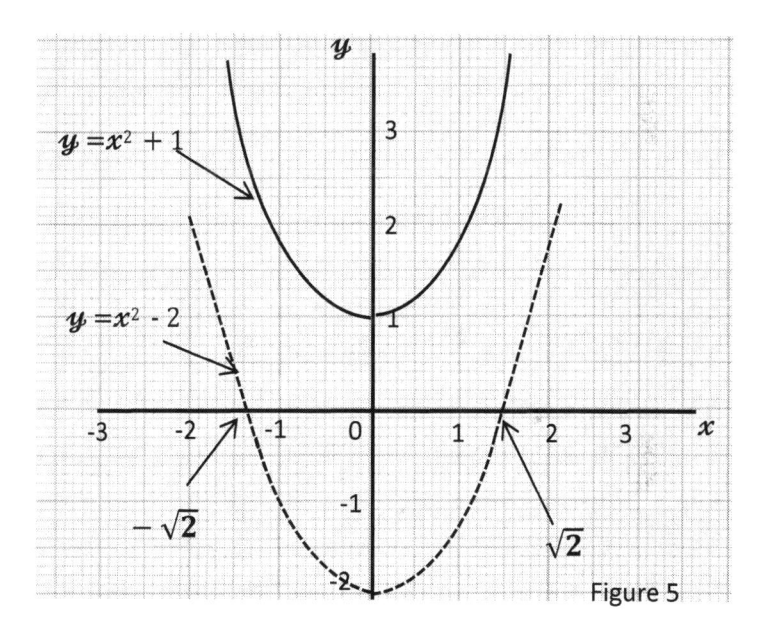

Figure 5

If a quadratic curve crosses the x axis it must always do it in two places. The values of x for which $y = 0$ are called **the solutions of the equation**.

They can also be referred to as the **roots** of the equation.

So, any equation $y = ax^2 + c$ will always have two solutions, that is two values of x for which $y = 0$. If the curve does **not** cross the x axis then the equation will have no solutions.

Key Stage 3 Maths Explained - Volume 2 Algebra

Finally, we can add a term in x to the quadratic equation. The equation now looks like this: $y = ax^2 + bx + c$. Quadratic curves with and without an x term are illustrated in Figure 6. The addition of this term with a positive coefficient **b** moves the curve down and to the left as shown in figure 7.

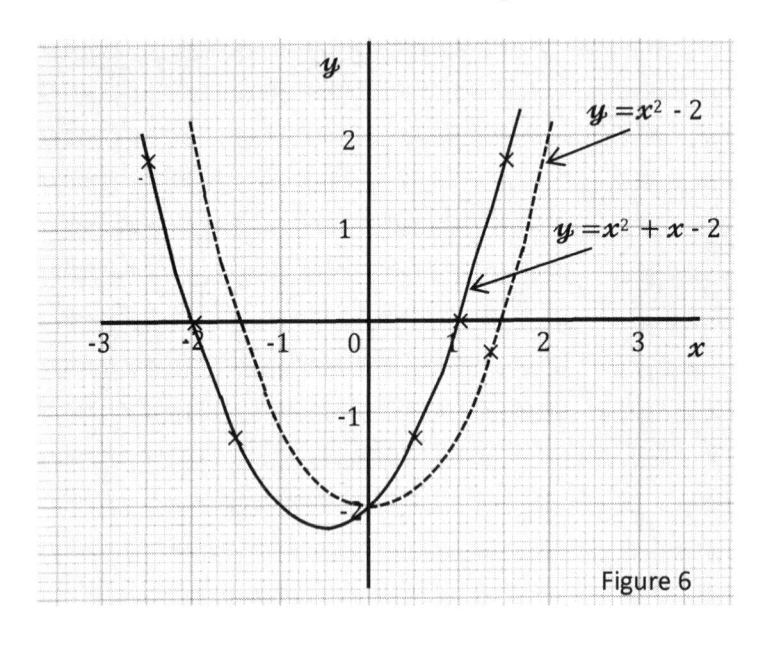

Figure 6

This table shows you the numbers used to plot the two curves in figure 6. In the curve, $y = x^2 + x - 2$
$y = 0$ when $x = +1$ and also when $x = -2$.

x	x^2	$y = x^2 - 2$	$y = x^2 + x - 2$
3	9	7	10
2	4	2	4
1	1	-1	0
0	0	-2	-2
-1	1	-1	-2
-1.5	2.25	0.25	-1.25
-2	4	2	0
-2.5	6.25	4.25	1.75

Chapter 23 – Graphs of Quadratic Equations

Parabolas

The curves drawn by quadratic equations are known as parabolas.

A parabola is an important shape. Parabolic mirrors are used in torches, in spot lights, in car headlights, and in the mirrors used in telescopes.

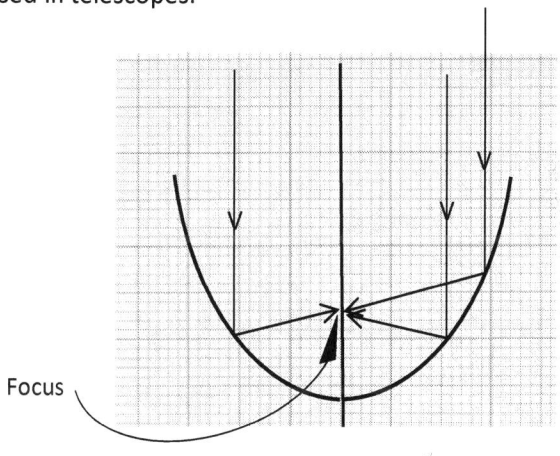

Focus

All the light coming from something a long way away, such as a star, is parallel. All parallel light is reflected by a parabolic mirror to a single point. This point is known as the **focus** of the mirror. A camera placed at the focus will see a clear image of the star.

(See chapter 33 for more about parallel lines)

Parabolic reflectors are used in radar antenna and in radio telescopes for exactly the same reason.

A source of high frequency radiation placed at the focus of a metal reflector can produce a parallel high-power radar beam.

Radio telescopes use large parabolic antenna to collect the maximum amount of radiation from a distant radio emitting star. This is all directed to the focus of the parabola and collected by a suitable radio detector

If a parabolic mirror is used in a torch or a spot light, then a small source of light (the filament of a bulb or a laser) at the focus of the mirror will produce a parallel beam of light.

If you move the light source a little towards the mirror the beam of light will spread out a little, if you move it past the focus the beam of light will converge, that is turn inwards towards the axis.

Chapter 23 – Graphs of Quadratic Equations

Exercise 23

Find an A4 sheet of graph paper.
Draw x and y axes as shown
Mark the x axis from -8 to +8
and y axes from -10 to +10. Make a table
With 4 columns. Head the first column x
and write +8, +7, ... to – 8 down the column.
With 0 half way down.

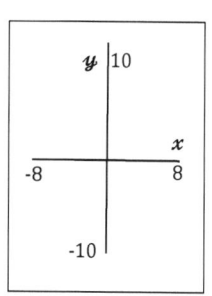

1) Head the next column $y = 0 \cdot 15x^2$ and enter all the values of y. Plot all the points and sketch a curve through them. Mark the curve as the graph of $y = 0 \cdot 15x^2$

2) Head the next column $y = 0 \cdot 15x^2 - 2$. Plot the points and draw the curve. Does the curve cross the x axis? Estimate the value of x at the crossing point.
2a) Estimate the values of x at the crossing point, when $y = 0$.

3) Head the last column $y = 0 \cdot 15x^2 + x - 2$. Plot the points and draw the curve. Does the curve cross the x axis?
3a) Estimate the values of x at the crossing point, when $y = 0$.

4) Draw the same axes and scales on another piece of graph paper. Make a table for values of x between -7 and +8 when $y^2 = x + 6$. Plot the points. Remember that for any number n, $n^2 =$ -n × -n as well as n × n.
4a) What happens when $x = -7$? What is y when $x = 0$?

5) Make a table for the value of x^2 and y^2 for the quadratic equation $x^2 + y^2 = 5^2$ for x values of between -5 and + 5. Draw the axes and plot the curve for values of x between -5 and +5.
5a) What shape have you drawn?
The answers are on the next page.

Key Stage 3 Maths Explained - Volume 2 Algebra

Answers to Exercise 26

x	Question 1 $y = 0\cdot15x^2$	Question 2 $y = 0\cdot15x^2 - 2$	Question 3 $y = 0\cdot15x^2 + x - 2$
8	9·6	7·6	15·6
7	7·35	5·35	12·35
6	5·4	3·4	9·4
5	3·75	1·75	6·75
4	2·4	0·4	4·4
3	1·35	−0·65	2·35
2	0·6	−1·4	0·6
1	0·15	−1·85	−0·85
0	0	−2	−2
-1	0·15	−1·85	-2·85
-2	0·6	−1·4	−3·4
-3	1·35	−0·65	−3·65
-4	2·4	0·4	−3·6
-5	3·75	1·75	−3·25
-6	5·4	3·4	−2·6
-7	7·35	5·35	−1·65
-8	9·6	7·6	−0·4

Chapter 23 – Graphs of Quadratic Equations

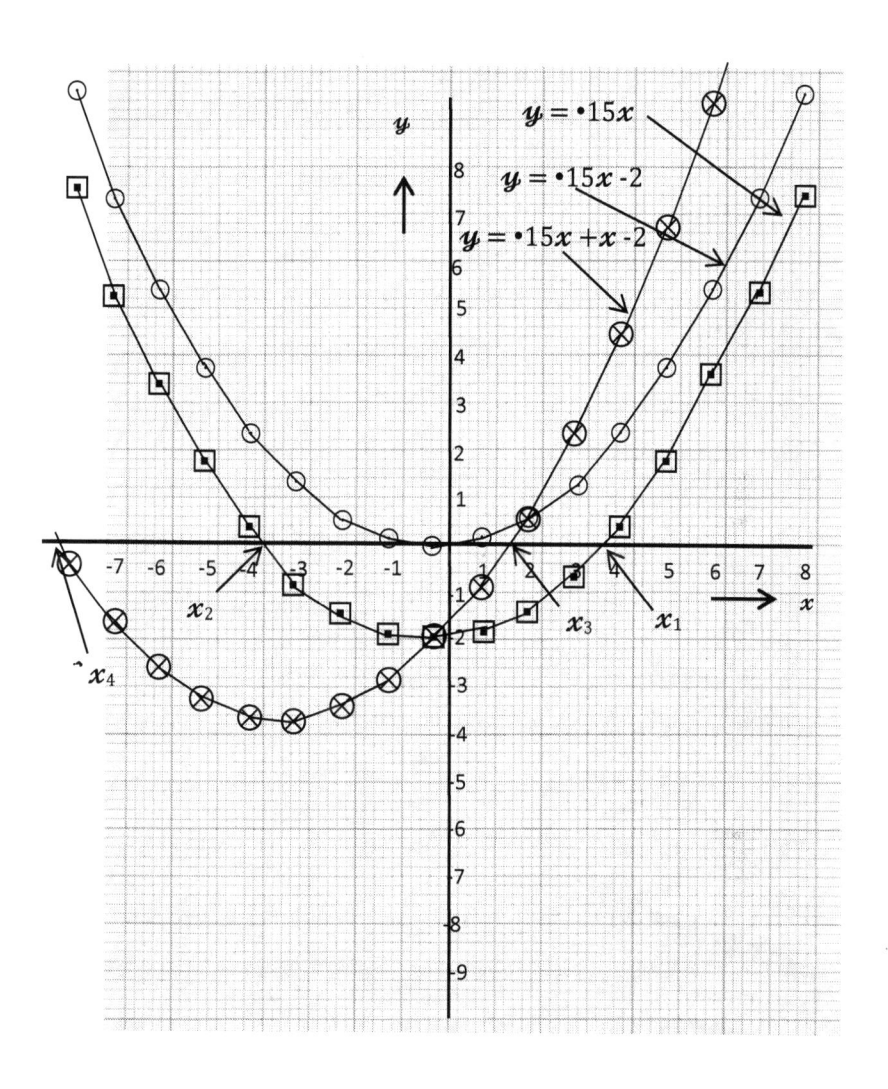

$y = \cdot15x$

$y = \cdot15x - 2$

$y = \cdot15x + x - 2$

2a) $y = 0$ when $x = +3\cdot65 = x_1$ and $x = -3\cdot65 = x_2$

3a) $y = 0$ when $x = +1\cdot61 = x_3$ and $x = -8\cdot28 = x_4$

Key Stage 3 Maths Explained - Volume 2 Algebra

4) Here is the table of values, in two sections:

x	−7	−6	−5	−4	−3	−2	−1	0
$y^2 = x + 6$	−1	0	1	2	3	4	5	6
$y =$	#	0	1	1·41	1·73	2	2·24	2.45
or $y =$	#	0	-1	−1·41	−1·73	−2	−·24	−2.45

x	1	2	3	4	5	6	7	8
$y^2 = x + 6$	7	8	9	10	11	12	13	14
$y =$	2.65	2·83	3	3·16	3·32	3·43	3·61	3·74
or $y =$	−2.65	−2·83	−3	−3·16	−3·32	−3·43	−3·61	−3·74

Chapter 23 – Graphs of Quadratic Equations

This is the curve

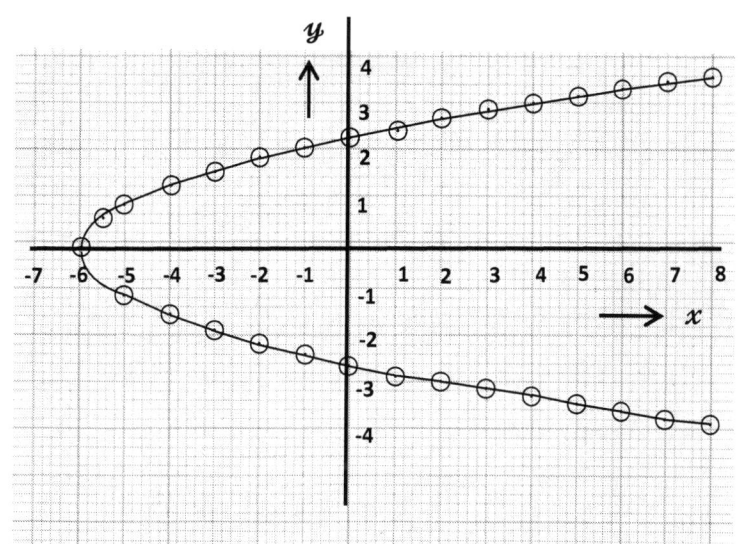

4a) The curve crosses the x axis at -6. There is no real number which is the square root of -7

5) Here is the table you should have worked out

x	x^2	$y^2 = 5^2 - x^2$	y
-5	25	0	0
-4	16	9	3 and -3
-3	9	16	4 and -4
-2	4	21	4•58 and –4•58
-1	1	24	4•90 and –4•90
0	0	25	5 and -5
1	1	24	4•90 and –4•90
2	4	21	4•58 and –4•58
3	9	16	4 and –4
4	16	9	3 and –3
5	25	0	0

And here is the curve

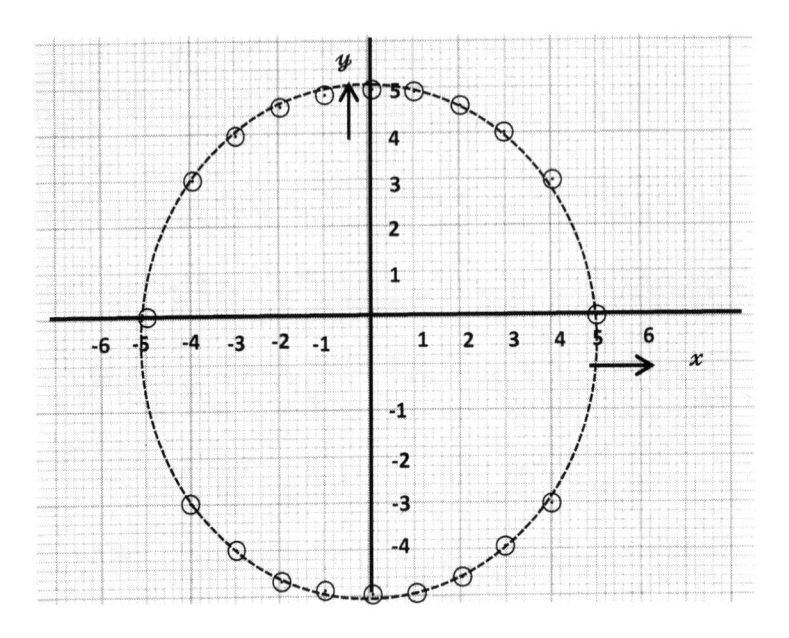

5a) You have drawn a circle.

Chapter 23 – Graphs of Quadratic Equations

Roots of Quadratic Equations

Questions 2 and 3 asked you to find the particular values of x which made $y = 0$, the values of x where the curves crossed the y axis.

Remember

These values are called **the Roots** of the quadratic equation.

Suppose you plotted the results of an experiment and find a curve which looks like a parabola. You know nothing else about the curve except that it crosses the y axis for two particular values of x (let us call them $x = x_1$ and $x = x_2$), and that when the curve crosses the y axis $x = 0$ and $y_1 = c$.

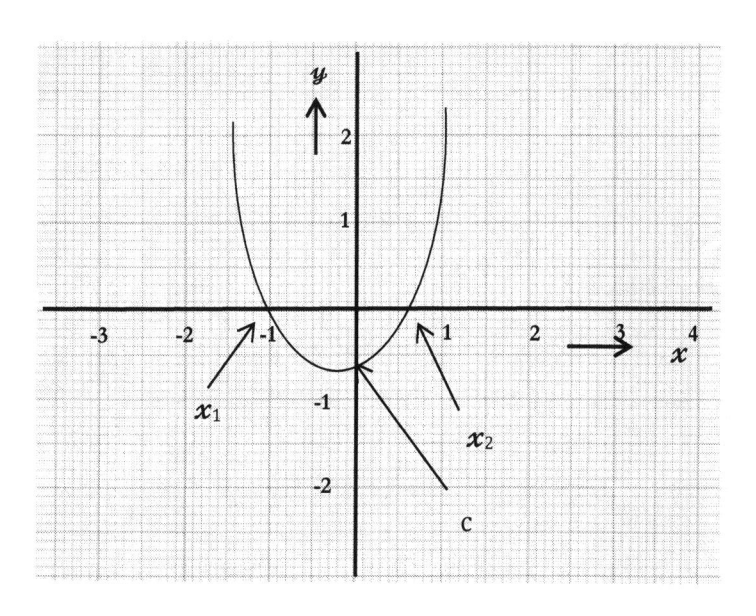

Key Stage 3 Maths Explained - Volume 2 Algebra

so $y = a(x - x_1)(x - x_2) = 0$.

When $x = x_1$ the first bracket is = 0,
and when $x = x_2$ the second bracket is = 0.

Now you can multiply the two brackets together just as you did in lesson 14. This gives $y = ax^2 - a(x_1 + x_2)x + ax_1x_2$.

The roots of this quadratic equation are x_1 and x_2. They are the two values of the variable x which make $y = 0$.

Finally, as the curve crosses the y axis at **c**. This is where $x = 0$

When $x = 0$, $\quad y = 0 - 0 + a(x_1x_2) = c$

So, the **a** in the equation, which we didn't know,

must be $a = \dfrac{c}{x_1x_2}$

Chapter 24 - Factors. What are they?

Factors

If you take $2x^2 + 3x + 4$ and multiply it by 5 you get $10x^2 + 15x + 20$.
So you have made 5 a factor of the expression $10x^2 + 15x + 20$
You can divide it by 5 and get back the original expression.

$$\frac{10}{5}x^2 + \frac{15}{5}x + \frac{20}{5} = 2x^2 + 3x + 4$$

So, 5 is a factor of $10x^2 + 15x + 20$.
Every number in that expression will divide by 5.
The two factors of $10x^2 + 15x + 20$ are 5 and $2x^2 + 3x + 4$

Here are some more expressions with factors:

$9y^2 + 6y + 3$, the factor is 3. $\frac{9}{3}y^2 + \frac{6}{3}y + \frac{3}{3} = 3y^2 + 2y + 1$

So, 3 goes exactly into $9y^2 + 6y + 3$

3 is a factor of $9y^2 + 6y + 3$, the other factor is $3y^2 + 2y + 1$

The factors must divide **exactly** into the whole expression.
No remainders or fractions are allowed.

Exercise 24

Find the factors in each of the expressions in this list: then divide by the factor to find the simplest form of each expression:

1) $4x^2 + 6x + 8$ 2) $5x^2 + 10x + 15$ 3) $6x^2 + 4x + 8$

4) $3x^2 + 9x - 6$ 5) $2x^2 + 8x - 10$ 6) $7x^2 + 14x - 21$

7) $4x^3 + 16x^2 - 4x + 8$ 8) $6x^3 + 3x^2 - 9x - 21$ 9) $8x^3 + 6x^2 - 4$

The answers are on the next page

Key Stage 3 Maths Explained - Volume 2 Algebra

Answers to Exercise 24:

1) $4x^2 + 6x + 8 = 2(2x^2 + 3x + 4)$ the factors are 2 and $(2x^2 + 3x + 4)$

2) $5x^2 + 10x + 15 = 5(x^2 + 2x + 3)$ the factors are 5 and $(x^2 + 2x + 3)$

3) $6x^2 + 4x + 8 = 2(3x^2 + 2x + 4)$ the factors are 2 and $(3x^2 + 2x + 4)$

4) $3x^2 + 9x - 6 = 3(x^2 + 3x - 2)$ the factors are 3 and $(x^2 + 3x - 2)$

5) $2x^2 + 8x - 10 = 2(x^2 + 4x - 5)$ the factors are 2 and $(x^2 + 4x - 5)$

6) $7x^2 + 14x - 21 = 7(x^2 + 2x - 3)$ the factors are 7 and $(x^2 + 2x - 3)$

7) $4x^3 + 16x^2 - 4x + 8 = 4(x^3 + 4x^2 - x + 2)$
the factors are 4 and $(x^3 + 4x^2 - x + 2)$

8) $6x^3 + 3x^2 - 9x - 21 = 3(2x^3 + x^2 - 3x - 7)$
the factors are 3 and $(2x^3 + x^2 - 3x - 7)$

9) $8x^3 + 6x^2 - 4 = 2(4x^3 + 3x^2 - 2)$
the factors are 2 and $(4x^3 + 3x^2 - 2)$

Chapter 25 - Multiplying Factors

Multiplying Factors

A factor does not have to contain just one number or one letter. Look carefully:

$4x^3 + 2x^2 + 6x$ has a common factor of $2x$

$2x \times 2x^2 + 2x \times x + 2x \times 3 = 2x(2x^2 + x + 3)$

$3x^4 + 9x^3 + 6x$ has a common factor of $3x$

$3x \times x^3 + 3x \times 3x^2 + 3x \times 2 = 3x(x^3 + 3x^2 + 2)$

This type of factor where the factor is found in each term, is called **a common factor,** as it is common to (or part of) all the terms.

Look at the last expression again.

$3x \times x^3 + 3x \times 3x^2 + 3x \times 2$ could be written as $3x(x^3 + 3x^2 + 2)$. If you multiply each of the terms in the bracket by $3x$ you get back to $3x^4 + 9x^3 + 6x$ again.

So, the $3x$ is a factor of $3x^4 + 9x^3 + 6x$. As it occurs in each term it is called a common factor; it is a factor of each term.

Exercise 25

Write these expressions as a common factor outside a bracket.

1) $7x^2 + 14x$ 2) $4x^3 + 6x^2 - 2x$ 3) $6x^3 - 9x$

4) $8x^3 + 6x^2$ 5) $4x^6 + 6x^4 - 2x^2$ 6) $7x^6 - 14x^4 - 21x^2$

The answers are on the next page

Answers to Exercise 25

1) $7x^2 + 14x = 7(x + 2)$ the factors are $7x$ and $(x + 2)$

2) $4x^3 + 6x^2 - 2x = 2(2x^2 + 3x - 1)$
    the factors are $2x$ and $(2x^2 + 3x - 1)$

3) $6x^3 - 9x = 3(2x^2 - 3)$ the factors are $3x$ and $(2x^2 - 3)$

4) $8x^3 + 6x^2 = 2x^2(4x + 3)$ the factors are $2x^2$ and $(4x + 3)$

5) $4x^6 + 6x^4 - 2x^2 = 2x^2(2x^4 + 3x^2 - 1)$
    the factors are $2x^2$ and $(2x^4 + 3x^2 - 1)$

6) $7x^6 - 14x^4 - 21x^2 = 7x^2(x^4 - 2x^2 - 3)$
    the factors are $7x^2$ and $(x^4 - 2x^2 - 3)$

Chapter 26 – Factors. Multiplying Brackets

Multiplying Brackets

Let's look at what happens when you multiply two brackets together. Suppose you take $(x + 3) \times (x + 4)$.

First, multiply the second bracket by the x from the first bracket
$$x(x + 4) = x^2 + 4x$$
Next multiply the second bracket by the 3 from the first bracket.

$$3(x + 4) = 3x + 12$$

Now add these answers together:

$$(x + 4)(x + 3) = x^2 + 3x + 4x + 12$$

So, the final result is: $(x + 3) \times (x + 4) = x^2 + 7x + 12$ —————— ①

Now take it to bits again.

If we put letters instead of numbers we have:

$(x + a)(x + b) = x^2 + ax + bx + ab$

So $(x + a)(x + b) = x^2 + (a + b)x + ab$. —————— ②

Now work this backwards: $x^2 = x \times x$. So, the first thing in both brackets must be x.

$$(x \quad)(x \quad)$$

Then as all the signs in the equation are positive, the signs in both brackets must be + so we have $(x + \;)(x + \;)$

Look at the terms in in equations ① and ②

Equation ① $(x + 4)(x + 3) = x^2 + 7x + 12$

Equation ② $(x + a)(x + b) = x^2 + (a + b)x + ab$

This shows two important results:

① **The coefficient** of x (that is the number multiplying x)
is (a + b)
② The number at the end (**the constant**) is a × b = ab

So going back to $x^2 + 7x + 12$, equation ①

$$a + b = 7$$
$$a \times b = 12$$

The equation now has two numbers which add up to 7, and which multiply to give 12.

a + b = 7	a × b = 12	
1 + 6 = 7	1 × 6 = 6	no
2 + 5 = 7	2 × 5 = 10	no
3 + 4 = 7	3 × 4 = 12	yes

Obviously, the two numbers which add up to give 7 and multiply to give 12 are 3 and 4.

So $x^2 + 7x + 12 = (x + 3)(x + 4)$

Chapter 26 – Factors. Multiplying Brackets

Here is another example, $x^2 + 6x + 8$

Try the numbers which add up to 6 and then find the pair of these which multiply to give 8.

a + b = 6	a × b = 8		
1 + 5	1 × 5 = 5	no	
2 + 4	2 × 4 = 8	yes	← This is the pair you need
3 + 3	3 × 3 = 9	no	

So, $x^2 + 6x + 8 = (x + 2)(x + 4)$

Key Stage 3 Maths Explained - Volume 2 Algebra

Now try this one: $x^2 + 5x - 24$. Here a + b is positive and a × b is negative.

a + b = 5	a × b = − 24	
6 − 1	−1 × 5 = − 6	no
7 − 2	−2 × 7 = −14	no
8 − 3	−3 × 8 = −24	yes ←This is the pair you need
9 - 4	-4 × 9 = -36	no

$(x + 8)(x - 3) = x^2 + 8x - 3x - 24 = x^2 + 5x - 24$.

So $x^2 + 5x - 24 = (x + 8)(x - 3)$

What about this? $x^2 - 7x - 44$. So a + b = −7 and a × b = − 44.

First find the factors of 44.
They are 1 and 44, or 2 and 22, or 4 and 11.

Only 4 and 11 have a difference of 7.

As a + b = 4 − 11 = −7, and a × b = 4 × −11 = − 44

Then $x^2 - 7x - 44 = (x + 4)(x - 11)$

With practice you will soon learn to spot the numbers without all this calculation.

Always check your answer.
$x^2 - 7x - 44 \quad = (x + 4)(x - 11)$
$\qquad\qquad\quad = x^2 + 4x - 11x + 4 \times -11$
$\qquad\qquad\quad = x^2 - 7x - 44$

Chapter 26 – Factors. Multiplying Brackets

Exercise 26

Factorize the following quadratics into brackets as $(x + a)(x + b)$
Find the values of a and b

Note: **a** and **b** are interchangeable.
It doesn't matter which way round you have them.

1) $x^2 + 7x + 12$

2) $x^2 + 7x + 10$

3) $x^2 + 9x + 8$

4) $x^2 + 11x + 28$

5) $x^2 + 9x + 18$

6) $x^2 + 13x + 42$

7) $x^2 + 11x + 18$

8) $x^2 + 9x + 20$

9) $x^2 + 15x + 56$

10) $x^2 + 12x + 32$

11) $x^2 - 9x + 18$

12) $x^2 + 2x - 35$

13) $x^2 + 5x - 24$

14) $x^2 + 7x - 18$

15) $x^2 + 3x - 28$

16) $x^2 + 2x - 15$

17) $x^2 + 5x - 36$

18) $x^2 + x - 30$

19) $x^2 + 5x - 14$

20) $x^2 + 2x - 48$

The answers are on the next page

Key Stage 3 Maths Explained - Volume 2 Algebra

Answers to Exercise 26

1) $(x + 3)(x + 4)$ a = 3, b = 4
2) $(x + 2)(x + 5)$ a = 2, b = 5
3) $(x + 8)(x + 1)$ a = 8, b = 1
4) $(x + 7)(x + 4)$ a = 7, b = 4
5) $(x + 3)(x + 6)$ a = 3, b = 6
6) $(x + 7)(x + 6)$ a = 6, b = 7
7) $(x + 2)(x + 9)$ a = 2, b = 9
8) $(x + 5)(x + 4)$ a = 5, b = 4
9) $(x + 7)(x + 8)$ a = 7, b = 8
10) $(x + 8)(x + 4)$ a = 8, b = 4
11) $(x - 6)(x - 3)$ a = -6, b = -3
12) $(x + 7)(x - 5)$ a = 7, b = -5
13) $(x + 8)(x - 3)$ a = 8, b = -3
14) $(x + 9)(x - 2)$ a = 9, b = -2
15) $(x + 7)(x - 4)$ a = 7, b = -4
16) $(x + 5)(x - 3)$ a = 5, b = -3
17) $(x + 9)(x - 4)$ a = 9, b = -4
18) $(x + 6)(x - 5)$ a = 6, b = -5
19) $(x + 7)(x - 2)$ a = 7, b = -2
20) $(x + 8)(x - 6)$ a = 8, b = -6

Chapter 27 – Using Linear Graphs to Solve Problems

Linear graphs can be used to solve problems.
Here is an example:

"At time = 0 a car is 1 mile away from a level crossing. It is being driven at 50 miles per hour. At the same time a train travelling at 90 miles per hour is 2.5 miles from the crossing. The gates will close fifteen seconds before the train gets to the crossing. "
1) Will the car or the train be the first to get to the crossing?
2) At what time will the car get to the crossing?
3) How far away from the crossing will the car be when the gates close?
4) How far away from the crossing is the train when the gates start to close?

To solve these questions, draw a graph to show how the car and train will move in the next two minutes.

Two minutes is 2 × 60 seconds. So, the table needs to show at least 120 seconds. There are 60 × 60 seconds = 3600 seconds in an hour. So, at 50 miles per hour, the distance car will be driven in 10 seconds

Is: $\dfrac{50 \times 10}{3600} = \dfrac{5}{36} = 0.1389$ miles in 10 seconds

So, the car travels 1·39 miles in 100 seconds.
At 100 seconds it will be 0·39 miles past the crossing.

At 90 miles per hour the train will go:

$\dfrac{90 \times 10}{3600} = \dfrac{9}{36} = \dfrac{1}{4} = 0.25$ miles in 10 seconds,

So, the train travels 2.5 miles in 100 seconds.

Now draw a graph like Figure 1 on the next page.

Key Stage 3 Maths Explained - Volume 2 Algebra

Unless you draw a very large graph your answers will only be accurate to about two significant figures but do draw the graphs as accurately as you can.

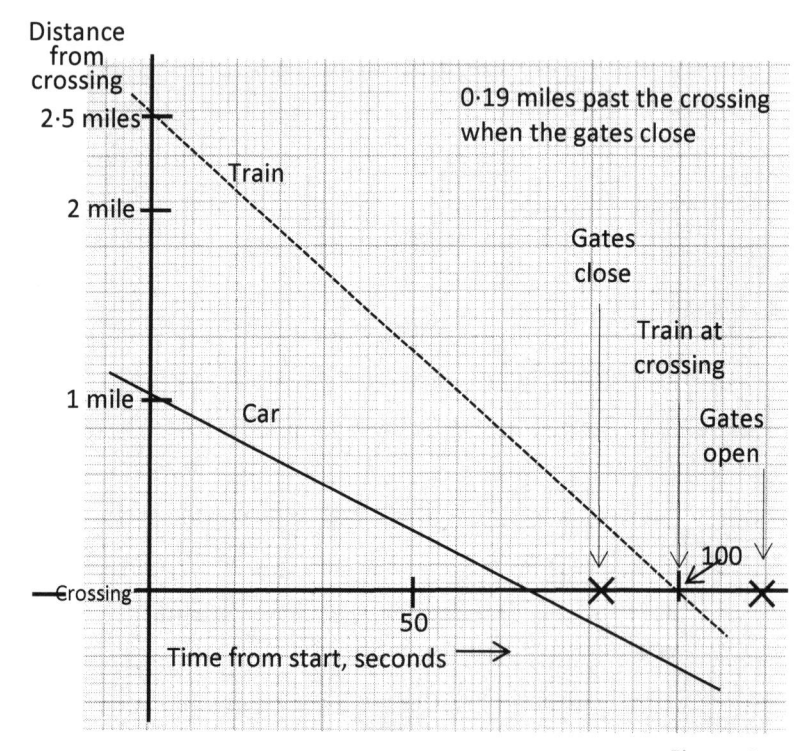

Figure 1

Now you can answer the questions.
1) The car actually gets to the crossing first.
2) It reaches the crossing 72 seconds after the start
2) The car is about 0·2 of a mile past the crossing when the gates close.
3) The train is 0·4 of a mile from the crossing when the gates start to close.

Chapter 28 – Using Graphs of Quadratics to Solve Problems

Here is another question which can be solved graphically.

"A boy is standing at the top of a vertical cliff which is 85 meters above sea level. He kicks a stone towards the sea. The stone flies out at 15 meters per second. Once over the edge of the cliff, the stone falls so that its height **h** above the sea is: $h = 85 - ½ \times 10 \times t^2$.
(Where the 10 is the acceleration due to gravity.)
Draw a graph which shows where the stone is at
0, 1, 2, 3, 4, 4·2 and 4·5 seconds after it is kicked.

Find:

    1) How long does it take the stone to hit the sea?

    2) How far out it is when it hits the sea?

Time, Seconds	$x = 15t$ meters	$h = 85 - 5t^2$ feet
0	0	85
1	15	80
2	30	65
3	45	40
4	60	5
4·2	63	-3·2
4·5	67·5	-16.25

Now you can draw the graph

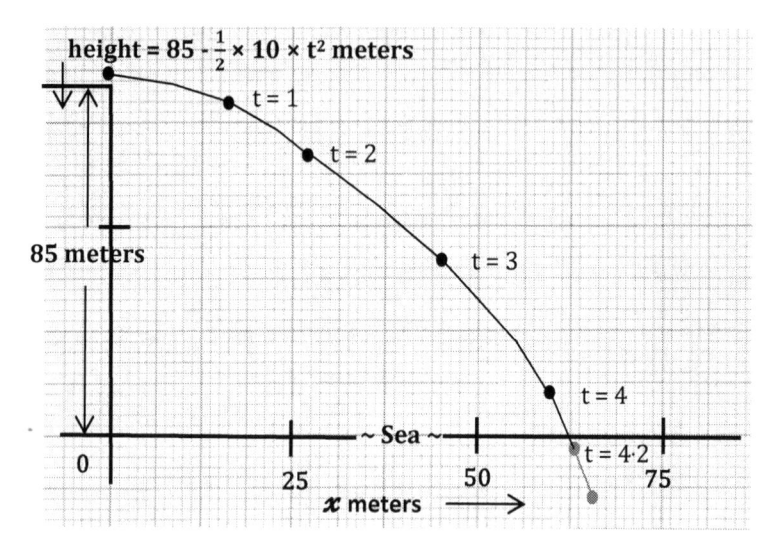

height = 85 - $\frac{1}{2}$ × 10 × t² meters

[Graph showing trajectory with points at t=1, t=2, t=3, t=4, t=4·2. Vertical axis marked 85 meters from 0. Horizontal axis marked in x meters at 25, 50 (Sea level), 75.]

From the graph we see that:

1) The stone hits the sea approximately 4·15 seconds after it is kicked.

2) It splashes about 62 meters out to sea.

Here is a third problem.

Two cars are travelling, one behind the other along a road. Their speed is 30m/s (67 miles per hour). The second car is 45 meters behind the first.
At t = 0, the driver of the first car sees something on the road and brakes hard. His car slows down by a_1 = 6 m/s every second. (This is really hard braking. Passengers would be thrown violently against the seat belts.)

The driver of the second car reacts ½ second later, but his tires are slightly more worn and his car slows down at only a_2 = 5 m/s every second. The distance travelled by either car when it is braking is s = 30t - ½at².

Chapter 28 – Using Graphs of Quadratics to Solve Problems

However, as the second car driver brakes ½ second after the first, for the second car you should use a different time t_2. For the second car the braking formula needs time $t_2 = t - ½$.

Make a table showing the time in seconds from 1 to 5 and the speed and distance travelled by both cars. Plot a graph with speed from 0 m/s to 30m/s on the y axis and distance travelled from -50 meters to +100 meters on the x axis. Use it to answer these questions:

1) How far will the first car travel before it stops.

2) How far will the second car travel?

3) Will the cars collide? What is the impact speed, or what is the final distance between the cars

Hint

Work out the position and speed of each car, before and after it starts to brake. There is no need to use more than one decimal place

Time	Speed of 1st car, m/s $V = 30 - 6t$	Position of 1st car, from start $s = 30t - ½6t^2$ m
0	30	0
0·5	27	14·25
1	24	27
2	18	48
3	12	63
4	6	72
4.5	3	74·75
5	0	75

Key Stage 3 Maths Explained - Volume 2 Algebra

Time t, Seconds	$t_2 = t - \frac{1}{2}$	Speed of 2nd car, m/s $V_2 = 30 - 6t_2$	Position of 2nd car, $s = -45 + 30t_2 - 5(t - \frac{1}{2})^2$ m
0	---	30	-45m
0·5	0	30	-30
1	0·5	27·5	-45 + 30 – 0·6 = -15.6
2	1·5	22·5	-45 + 60 – 5·6 = 9·4
3	2·5	17·5	-45 + 90 – 15·6 = 29·4
4	3·5	12·5	-45 + 120 – 30·6 = 44·4
5	4·5	7·5	-45 + 150 – 50·6 = 54·4
6	5·5	2·5	-45 + 180 - 75.6 = 59.4
6·5	6	0	-45 + 195 - 90 = 60

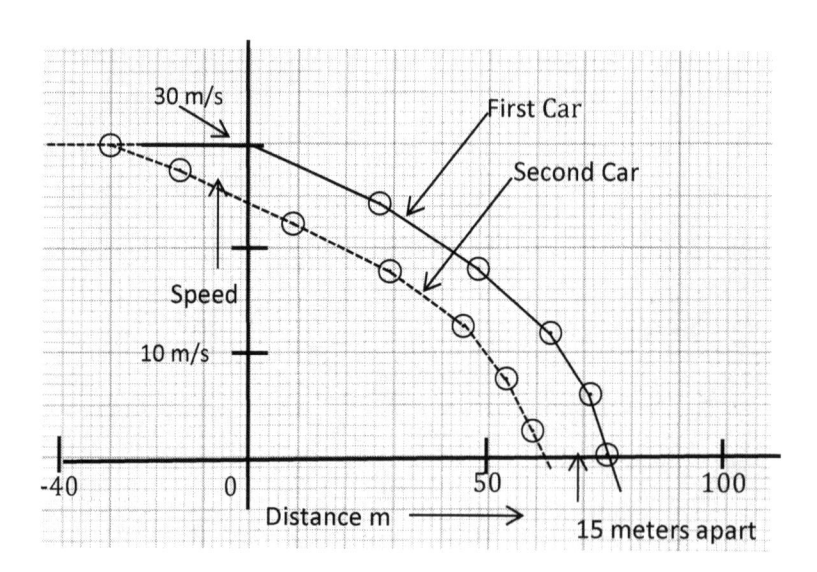

From the graph we can see that:
1) From the time it starts braking, the first car travels 75 meters before it stops.
2) The second car is 45 meters behind the first and travels 45m + 63 = 108m before it stops.
3) The second car stops 15 meters behind the first car.

Chapter 28 – Using Graphs of Quadratics to Solve Problems

We assumed that the driver of the second car was alert, had fast reactions and started to brake within half a second. Now see what would happen if it took him a full second to start to brake!

Time t, Seconds	$t_2 = t_2$	Speed of 2nd car, m/s $V_2 = 30 - 5t_2$	Position of 2nd car, $s = -45 + 30t_1 - 2·5(t_2)^2$ m
0	---	30	-45m
0·5	---	30	-45 + 15 = -30
1	0	30	-45 + 30 = -15
2	1	25	-45 + 60 – 2·5 = +12·5
3	2	20	-45 + 90 – 10 = 35
4	3	15	-45 + 120 – 22·5 = 52·5
5	4	10	-45 + 150 – 40 = 65
6	5	5	-45 + 180 – 62·5 = 72.5
7	6	0	-45 + 210 - 90 = 75
8	7	0	75

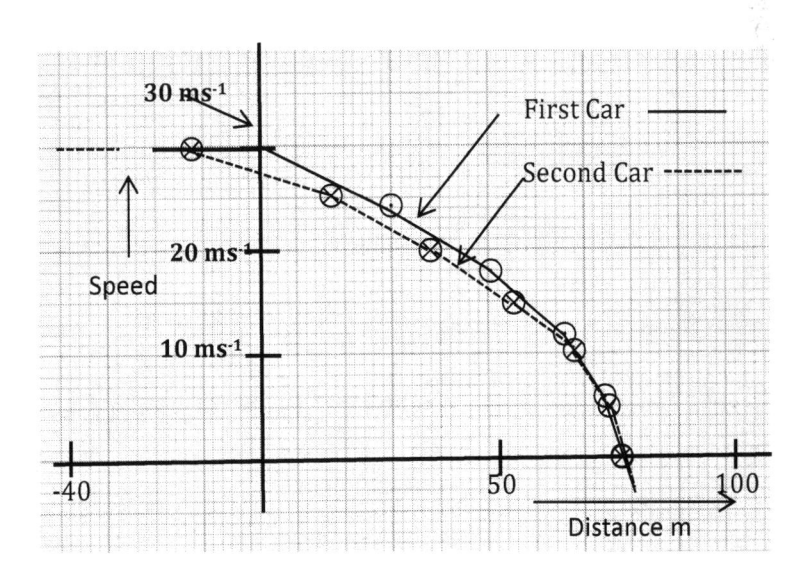

Key Stage 3 Maths Explained - Volume 2 Algebra

As you can see, the situation is now much more serious. With the slightly longer reaction time the two cars end up colliding. Three seconds after the first car brakes they are 20 meters apart, but the first car comes to a halt 6 seconds after it started braking and the second car runs into the back of it 1 second later.

Now do exercise 28

Exercise 28

1) A boy kicks a ball across a field. The ball flies out at 12 meters per second and upwards at 12 meters per second,

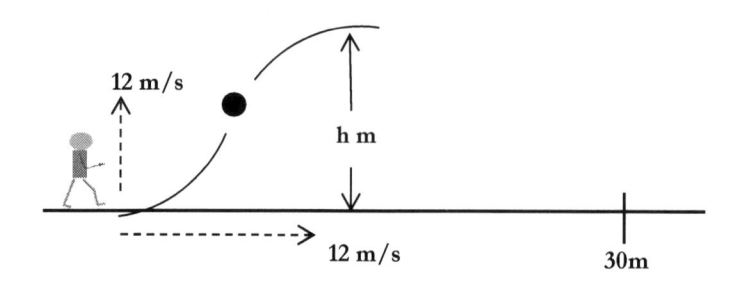

but gravity will make the ball start to fall at ½ × 10t² m/s
So that the equation for the height of the ball above the field is
h = 12t – 5t² meters. Plot a graph to show where the ball is at
t = 0· 5, 0·8, 1·0s, 1·3, 1·5, 1·7, 2·0, 2·5, and 2.8 seconds after it has been kicked. Show both height and distance.

Use your graph to:

a) estimate the maximum height to which the ball goes,
b) the time after kicking that it starts to go down,
c) the distance it reaches at the first bounce, and
d) the time at which it bounces.

(give your answers to 1 decimal place)

Chapter 28 – Using Graphs of Quadratics to Solve Problems

Question 2)

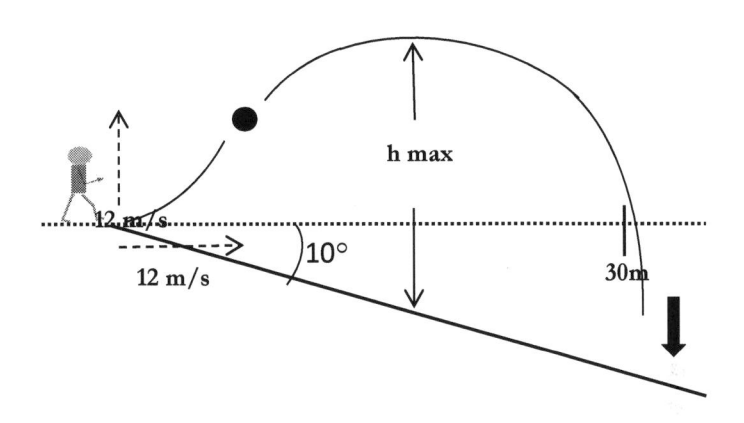

This time the field slopes down at 10° as shown.

Taking a ruler vertically along your graph:

a) Estimate the time when the ball's height above the sloping surface is greatest,

b) estimate the greatest height, **h max**, above the sloping surface reached by the ball.

c) estimate the time when the ball first bounces on the sloping surface,

d) estimate the distance down the slope when the ball first bounces.

Give your answers to the nearest 0·1 second and to the nearest meter

Key Stage 3 Maths Explained - Volume 2 Algebra

Answers to Exercise 28

1) $h = 12t - 5t^2$ meters $s = 12t$ meters

t	0·5	0·8	1·0	1·3	1·5	1·7	2·0	2·5	2·8
h	4·75	6·4	7·0	7·2	6·75	6	4·0	-1·25	-7·15
s	6	9·6	12	15·6	18	20·4	24	30	33·6

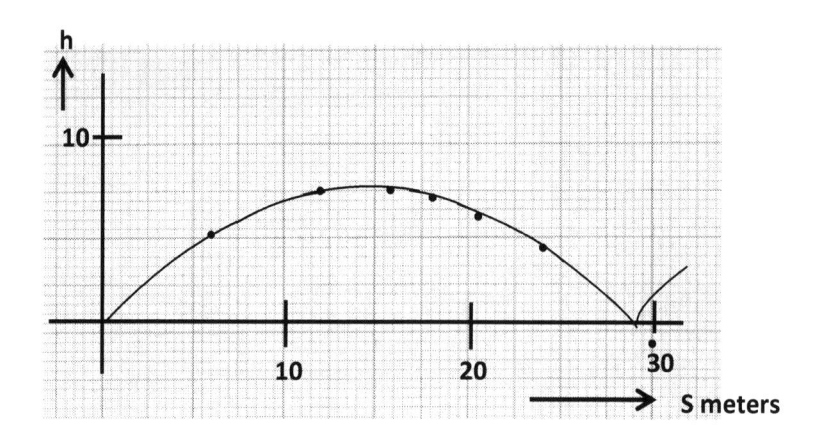

a) Its maximum height is 7·2 meters

b) The ball starts to go down after 1·2 seconds

c) The first bounce occurs at 2.9 seconds,

d) at a distance of 28.6 meters from the boy

Give your answers to the nearest 0·1 seconds, and to the nearest meter.

Chapter 28 – Using Graphs of Quadratics to Solve Problems

2)

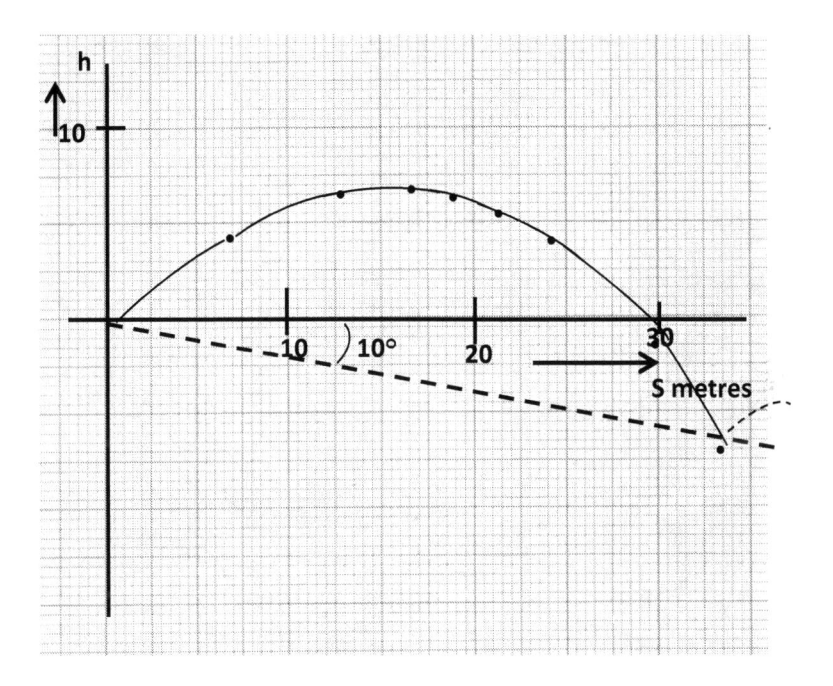

h
10

-10 10° 20 30
          S metres

(The answers you to be found from this graph are given on the next page)

Answers to question 2:

The curve is the same shape as in question 1, but the field now slopes down at 10° so the answers will be different.
In this case:

a) the maximum height above the sloping surface is 11m

b) this occurs 1.5 seconds after the ball is kicked.

c) the first bounce occurs 2·93 seconds after the ball is kicked

d) the ball bounces 38 meters down the sloping surface.
(any answer within 0·1 seconds and 1 meter of these answers is acceptable)

Chapter 29 – Exponential Graphs

In exponential graphs the x is an index.

So $y = n^x$ is an exponential function. Chapter 5 of this volume and Chapter 35 of the first volume looked at the way we can use indices. Here is a reminder of these rules.

Rules for Indices

Rule 1. When you multiply two powers of the same number together you add the indices. For example, if n, a and b are any numbers: $n^a \times n^b = n^{a+b}$

This was illustrated by $n^3 \times n^2 = n \times n \times n \times n \times n = n^5 = n^{(3+2)}$

Rule 2. When you divide two powers of the same number you subtract the indices: $n^a \div n^b = n^{a-b}$

This was illustrated by $n^3 \div n^2 = \dfrac{n \times n \times n}{n \times n} = n^{(3-2)} = n^1 = n$

It follows that $n^{-a} = \dfrac{1}{n^a}$

Rule 3. Any number with an index of 0 has a value of 1.
$n^a \div n^a = n^{a-a} = n^0 = 1$, whatever the value of n and a

Rule 4. To raise an expression with powers in it to a higher power, you multiply the indices inside the bracket by the index outside the bracket. In chapter 5 this was illustrated by:
$(n^4)^3 = n^4 \times n^4 \times n^4 = n^{4+4+4} = n^{4 \times 3} = n^{12}$

Rule 5 Fractions in indices mean the same as taking roots.
$n^{½} = \sqrt{n}$. This is illustrated by: $10^{½} \times 10^{½} = 10^{½ + ½} = 10^1 = 10$

So $n^{\frac{1}{m}} = \sqrt[m]{n}$, the mth root of n.

Key Stage 3 Maths Explained - Volume 2 Algebra

All this should be revision.

Now look at the meaning of the algebraic equation: $y = n^x$

As an example make n = 2, and plot the graph of

$y = 2^x$ for x = 0, 1, 2, 3, The '2' is called the **Base**.

Curves like this are called **Power Curves** because the **base number** (in this case 2) is raised to **a power** (in this case x). They prove to be extremely useful. Suppose you want to multiply 2.3 by 3.6 and don't have a calculator. You can draw one horizontal line from y = 2.3 to the line on your graph.

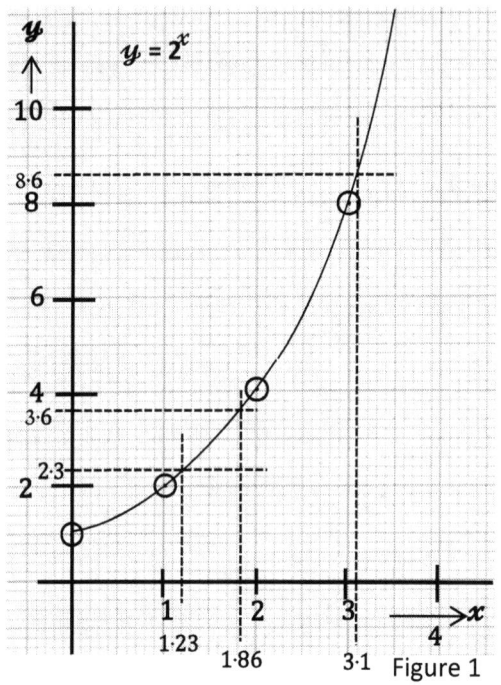

Watch out! in this figure the x and y scales are not the same

Figure 1

Then draw another line straight down to the x axis and find that it corresponds to x = 1·23. Then you draw another horizontal line from y = 3·6 to your curve. Then go straight down to the x axis and find that it corresponds to x = 1·86. When you multiply two numbers together you add the indices. So 2·3 × 3·6 = $2^{(1·23+1·86)}$ = $2^{3·10}$

Now plot a line up from x = 3·10 to the curve and find that it corresponds to y = 8·6. You have exchanged a long multiplication for an easier addition sum.

Chapter 29 – Exponential Graphs

In practice, if you want to use this method you would have to plot your graph very accurately on a large sheet of graph paper. Before calculators were invented this method was regularly used, it is called "multiplication by the use of logarithms". However, it is normally used with powers of 10 not powers of 2. It is called **multiplication by the use of logarithms to the base 10**. Instead of a curve, you can use a set of tables with four decimal places. (Seven decimal places give more accurate answers.)

Power curves like the one in Figure 1 can be plotted for any base number not just for 2 or 10. There is an <u>irrational number</u> 2.718278⋯, called "The exponential" and known by the letter **e** which is often used as the base for power curves. This is because its slope of $y = e^x$ is everywhere the same as its value. It is usually used in the form $y = e^{-x}$ (with a negative sign in front of the x). The curve is plotted in figure 2.

The numbers after the decimal point go on for ever

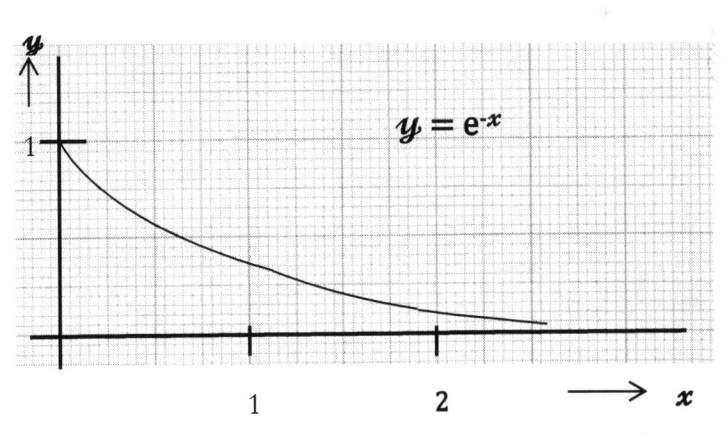

$y = e^{-x}$

Figure 2

Many things in nature follow negative power curves.
If you open the sluice in a canal lock, figure 3, the water level drops quickly at first and then more slowly. This is because the rate at which the water flows out of the lock depends on the pressure pushing it out, and this depends on the height of the water.

Key Stage 3 Maths Explained - Volume 2 Algebra

Figure 3

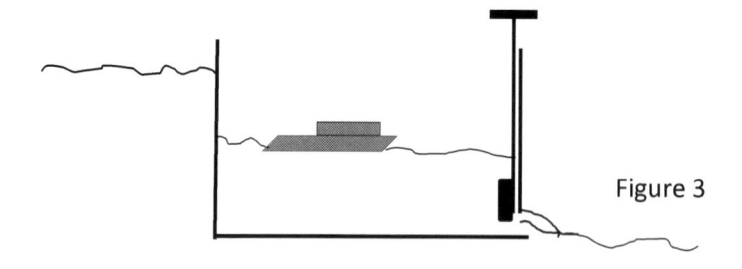

The pressure depends on the difference in height between the water level in the lock and the level outside. The pressure falls as the water level drops. This might go on forever as the water levels in, and on the lower side, will never be exactly the same, but when they are fairly close, the level of the ripples on the water will become more important; or someone will open the lock gates and the flow will stop.

Many other natural things, such as the discharge of batteries, and deflating balloons follow this sort of negative power law. In mathematics quantities which obey negative power laws go on to infinity getting ever smaller but never actually falling quite to zero.

Some things grow according positive power laws. Examples are explosions. Explosions start as something burning, in an enclosed space. The pressure increases rapidly. As the pressure gets bigger so does the rate at which the explosive burns. Finally, the bomb case bursts.

Here is another example of a positive power law. Locusts, a sort of tropical grasshopper, can hatch from eggs and grow very quickly. If conditions are right, a small number of these insects, each laying many eggs, can increase to many billions in a few months. The numbers of insects increase as a power law. Then the swarm of insects eats every green leaf they can find. They then fly over the land eating every growing thing, their numbers increasing all the time as a positive power law. Eventually, when they have eaten everything they can find, most of them will die of starvation and their numbers will collapse down again.

Chapter 30 – Reciprocal Graphs

Figure 1 **is a reciprocal graph**. It is a graph of $y = \dfrac{1}{x}$

This graph is called a **Rectangular Hyperbola**
It is rectangular because it fits into a pair of rectangular axes.

Figure 1

You can have other (not rectangular) axes (figure 2)

Hyperbolae go to infinity along each axis. They never quite touch their axes.

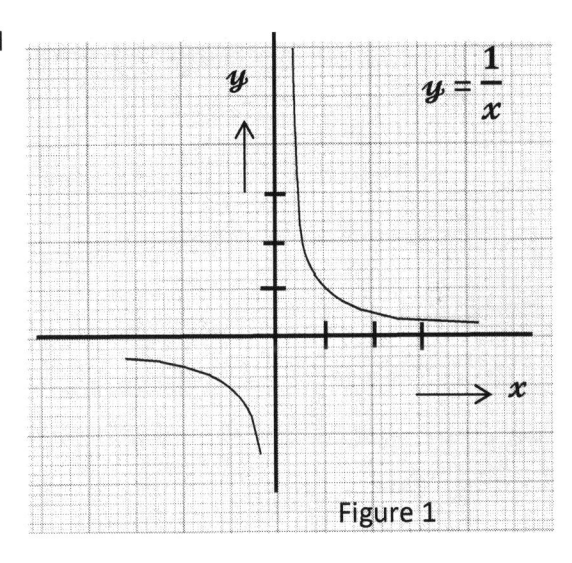

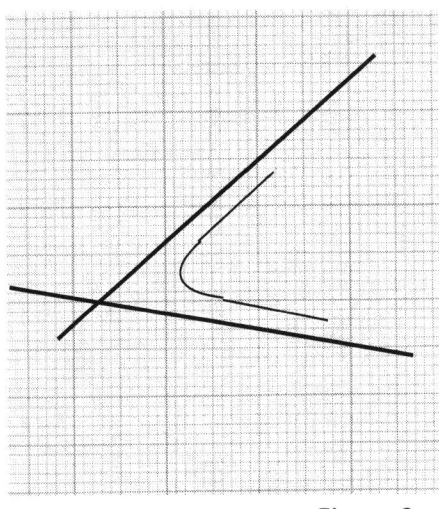

Figure 2

Key Stage 3 Maths Explained - Volume 2 Algebra

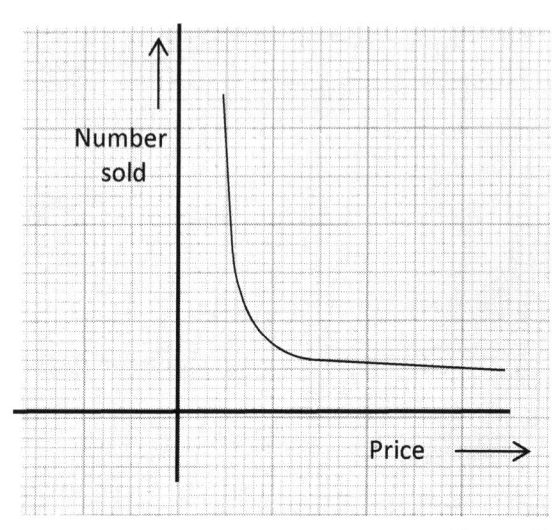

[Graph showing a rectangular hyperbola with "Number sold" on y-axis and "Price" on x-axis]

Figure 3

Economists use these graphs to explain how the number of items sold changes with the price charged, figure 3. They plot price on the x axis and number sold on the y axis. You will sell a lot, if the price is very low (small value of x) and will sell hardly any, if the price is much higher (large value of x)

This sort of graph also occurs in physics and engineering.
 For example, if you compress a gas its volume will get smaller; $V = \frac{RT}{P}$ (Volume of gas = the gas constant, R ×Temperature, divided by pressure p)
Again, the current (I) flowing through the heating element of an electric fire is inversely proportional to its resistance (**R**).
$I = \frac{V}{R}$. The resistance increases as the element heats up making the current smaller. (Here V is the voltage across the resistor). The relationship between current and resistance is again a rectangular hyperbola.
There is no exercise on this chapter.

Chapter 31 - Geometry - Lines and Angles

Your ruler gives you the ability to draw straight lines.

Where two lines meet or cross you get **angles.**

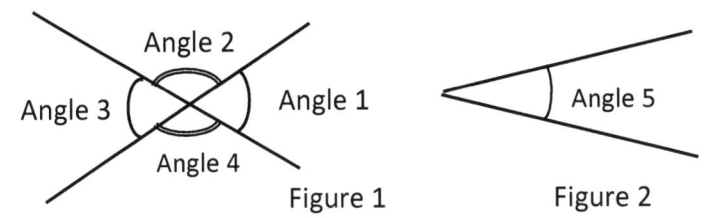

Figure 1   Figure 2

Figure 1 shows two lines which make 4 angles where the two lines cross. Figure 2 shows one angle where two lines meet at a point. Angles are measured in degrees which are shown by a very small circle at the top of the number; for example 20° (twenty degrees) or 5° (five degrees).

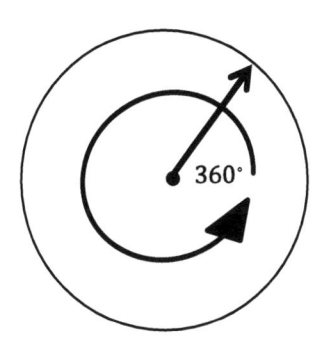

The angle that the hands of a clock trace out in one complete turn is 360°. So if it only goes half way round it turns through $\frac{360°}{2} = 180°$.

So, the angle at the center of a circle is 360°, and at a point on a straight line the angle is 180°,

Key Stage 3 Maths Explained - Volume 2 Geometry

You must be able to **measure angles** accurately. **Protractors** measure angles. They come in two sizes, 180° and 360°.

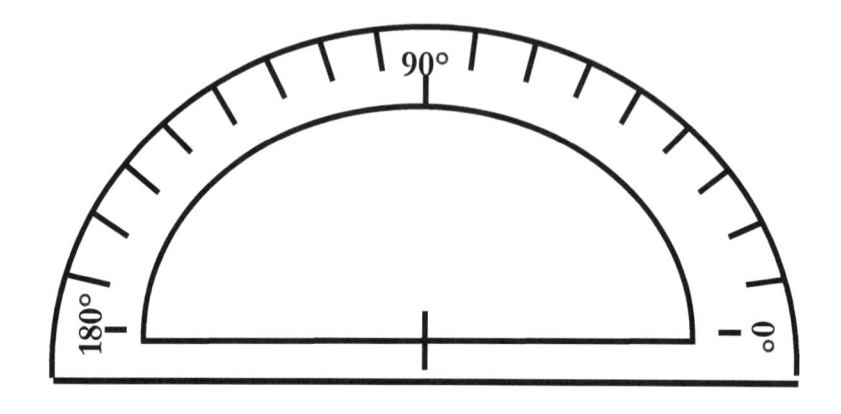

Protractor

All protractors are graduated in degrees.

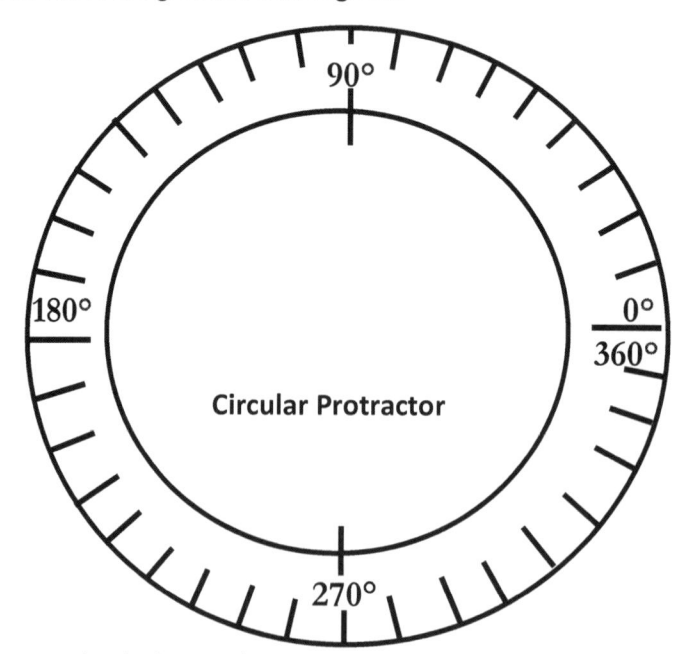

Circular Protractor

The convention is that angles are positive in an anti-clockwise direction

Chapter 31 - Geometry - Lines and Angles

Protractors have two scales. One goes from 0° on the left to 180° on the right. The other goes in the opposite direction

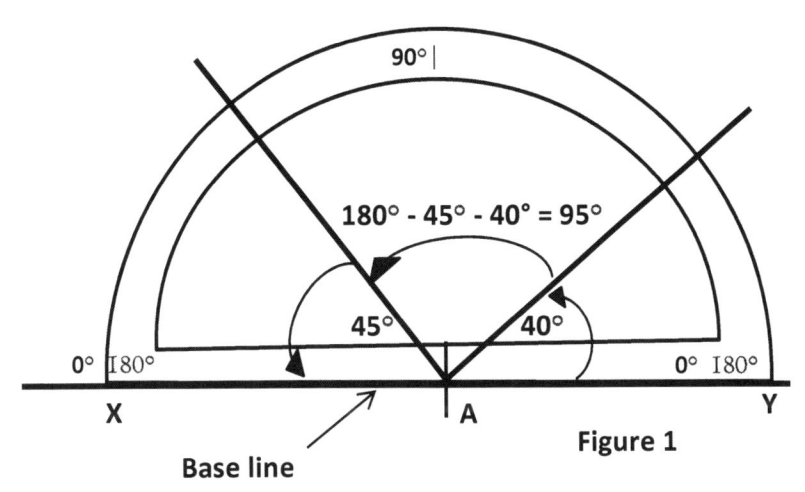

Figure 1

Base line

This allows you to measure angles on both sides of the point A. One starts with 0° at **X** and the other with 0° at **Y**.

You have to be very careful about measuring angles. Suppose you want to measure the angle ∠**EAC** in figure 2. (The sign ∠ shows that there is an angle. The letters EAC tell you that it is the angle where the line EA meets line DC at point A.) Put the bottom of the protractor on the line **CD** with its center mark exactly over **A**. Use the scale with 0° near **C** and see where the line **EA** comes to on that scale, marked **B**. This reads 48 so the angle ∠**EAC** is 48°.

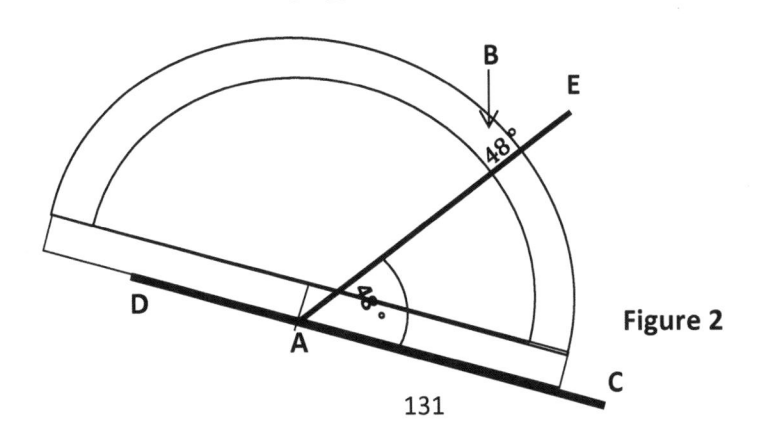

Remember.

Figure 2

131

Key Stage 3 Maths Explained - Volume 2 Geometry

Before you can do any calculations, you have to have some numbers. Most of the numbers in Geometry come from measuring lines and angles. These lines and angles form shapes: some are one dimensional, some are two dimensional, and some have three dimensions.

A line has one dimension. It goes from one point to another.

A ——————— B

The **straight line** is the **shortest path** from A to B. If the line goes by a longer way round it is still a line, but it will be longer and now occupies two dimensions.

An area has two dimensions. It can be a square, a circle, any shape. It can, be like a carpet on the floor, it can cover the floor.

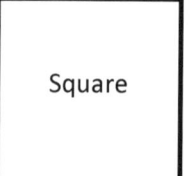

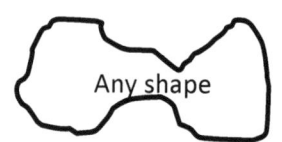

Square

Any shape

A volume has three dimensions. As this page has only two, it is difficult to show a three-dimensional figure. This is how we draw a cube. So, we can, with care, show a three-dimensional object.

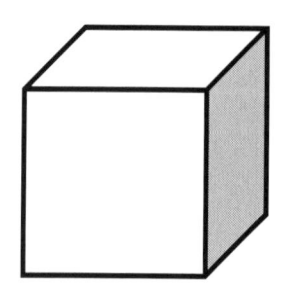

However, in the first stages of geometry we only deal with two dimensions.

Chapter 32 – Drawing Tools

Drawing Tools

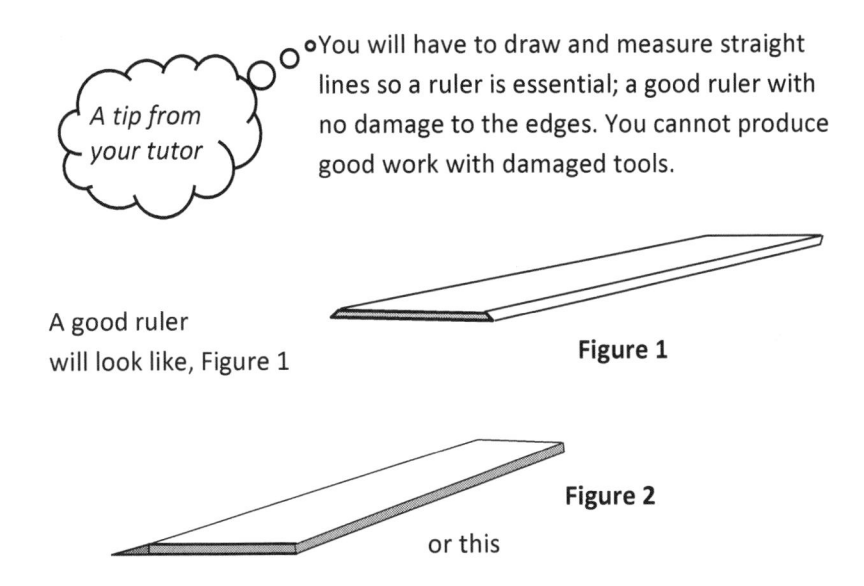

A tip from your tutor

You will have to draw and measure straight lines so a ruler is essential; a good ruler with no damage to the edges. You cannot produce good work with damaged tools.

A good ruler will look like, Figure 1

Figure 1

Figure 2

or this

The sloping side or sides will enable you to put the scale exactly on the line you are measuring. Acccurate measurements give good answers!

To use a ruler accurately to measure a length there are three steps.

1. Make sure that the first line, the zero mark, on the ruler is exactly on the start of the line you are measuring. (See figure 3)

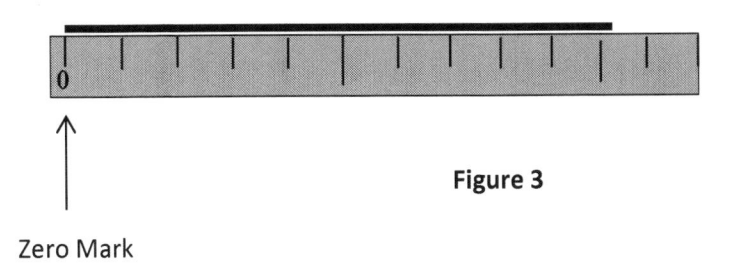

Figure 3

Zero Mark

Key Stage 3 Maths Explained - Volume 2 Geometry

2) Position your eye directly over the other end of the line
This sounds simple, but if you are not looking straight down you can get an inaccurate measurment.

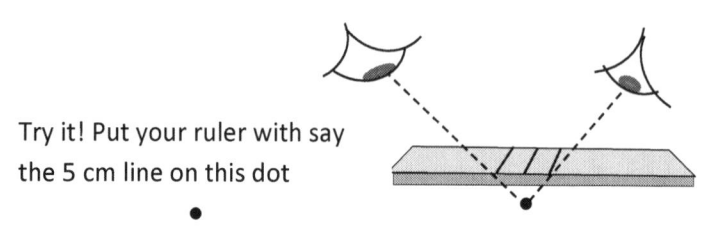

Try it! Put your ruler with say the 5 cm line on this dot

Figure 1

Now <u>move</u> your head <u>sideways</u> and you will see that the dot can be half way between the 4.9 and the 5 cm marks, or half way between the 5 and the 5·1 cm marks.

Using your tools properly will get you better marks, as your results will be more accurate. More importantly still, you will learn to do things well so that you will be satisfied with your work.

Care over taking measurements applies to using protractors as well.

The last tip is to use a sharp pencil to produce a small dot. · A blunt pencil produces a small blob ● This blob is 1 mm across.

A   B

A B can be anything between 3·9 cm to 4·1 cm. Depending on how you look down on the ruler. Try it!

Look after your tools. Use them carefully. It takes very little extra time, 1 or 2 seconds, and you will get higher marks, and understand what you are doing.

Chapter 33 – Planes, Parallel Lines and Right Angles

The parallel lines, right angles and **circles** described in these chapters are all drawn on a flat surface, like a sheet of paper. This extends as far as you need it in all directions without edges or folds. This sort of geometry is called **Plane Geometry.**

Geometry was devised to help people measure out fields for farms and lay out buildings. The word Geo means Earth and geometry means measuring things on the earth.

In Plane Geometry **parallel lines** are lines, like railway lines, which never cross however far you extend them. (If you let the distance between railway lines change the train would fall off.)

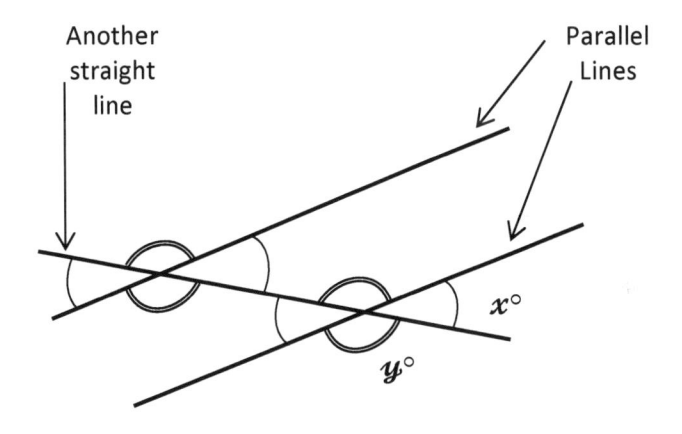

If another straight line is drawn across a pair of parallel lines then all the four angles marked with a single curve are the same. This is true whatever their size and however far the two parallel lines are apart.

Since the angles on any straight line must add up to 180°,
$x° + y° = 180°$

It must be true that all the four angles marked with double lines are also equal.

Key Stage 3 Maths Explained - Volume 2 Geometry

A right angle is an important angle. In Figure 2 two lines, AB and CD are at right angles to one another.

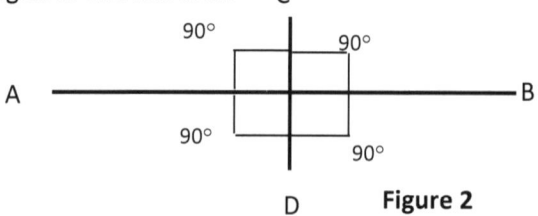

```
          C
          90°
               90°
A ─────────┼───────── B
          90°
               90°
          D      Figure 2
```

The angles between them are all equal: 90° (ninety degrees) which is a quarter of a full circle.

Line CD is said to be **normal** or **perpendicular** to the line AB.

A right angle, which is another name for a 90° angle is marked with a square sign as shown in Figure 3.

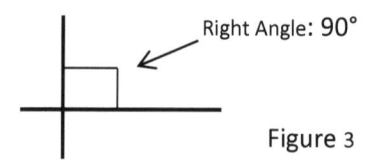

Right Angle: 90°

Figure 3

You can draw the line CD and make it normal (at right angles) to AB using compass (Figure 4)

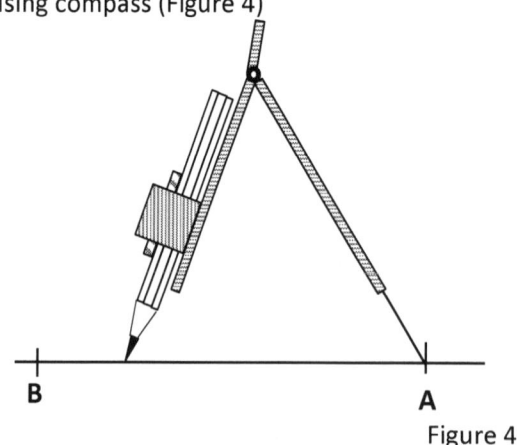

B   A
Figure 4

To do this, stick the point of your compass into point A. Open your compass until the pencil point goes a little beyond the mid-point between A and B. Draw an arc which goes either side of AB (Figure 5)

Chapter 33 – Planes, Parallel Lines and Right Angles

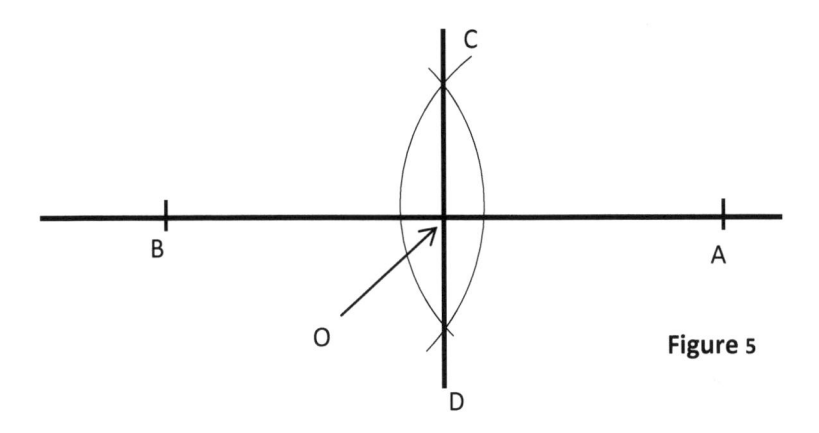

Figure 5

Now stick the point of your compass into point B, taking care not to change the angle of your compass. Draw another arc which goes either side of your line. Now draw a line CD through the points where the arcs cross above and below the line. Line CD is now at right angles to AB. Line CD can also be described as **normal** to AB.

Line CD **bisects** the distance between point A and point B; that is, it divides AB into 2 equal parts. The lines AO and OB are the same length. The lengths AO = OB.

Also, point O where the two lines cross is exactly half way between A and B. This is a most important method. Draftsmen use it to construct right-angles in drawings. Surveyors use the same method (with pegs in the ground and a long tape measure to mark out the arcs), to make sure the foundations of the walls are at right-angles to each another.

Key Stage 3 Maths Explained - Volume 2 Geometry

Pencil compasses can also be used to **bisect** any angle (that is to divide an angle into two equal parts). Here are two lines which cross at **A**, making an angle $x°$, (Figure 6).

To bisect the angle $x°$, stick the point of your compasses into point **A**, and draw two short arcs across the two lines, without changing the compass angle.

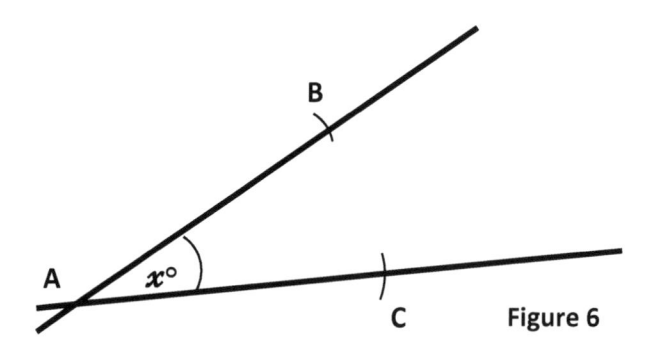

Figure 6

Now stick the point of your compasses into point B and draw another arc roughly half way between the two lines. Move the point of your compasses to **C**, and draw a fourth arc. The two new arcs cross at **D**.

Draw a line through **A** and **D**. This line divides the angle x (or bisects it) into two equal angles each of $\frac{x°}{2}$ as shown in Figure 7. This construction **bisects** the angle $\angle$BAC. Angle $\angle$BAD = $\angle$DAC

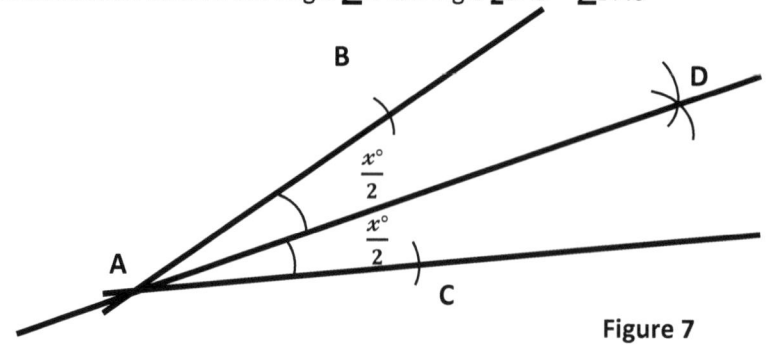

Figure 7

138

Chapter 33 – Planes, Parallel Lines and Right Angles

> **Note:** You can't divide a line or angle into three equal parts using a ruler and compasses. To construct an angle of 30° draw an equilateral triangle (three equal angles and three sides of the same length) and bisect one of the 60° angles. To make a 15° angle bisect one of the 30° angles.

Exercise 31 to 33

You will need a sheet of clean A4 paper, a sharp pencil, a ruler, some pencil compasses and a protractor, and perhaps a rubber.

Draw a horizontal line 15cm long about 10 cm above the bottom of the piece of A4 paper. Mark two points about 1 cm from either end. Label them **A** and **B**. Now use your pencil compasses to bisect the line AB. Draw a vertical line, about 12cm long, through the midpoint of your line **AB**. Label the top of the line **C** and the bottom of the line **D**. Label the point where the two lines cross **O**. Use your compasses to bisect (that is to divide in two equal parts) the angle ∠COB. Draw the line which bisects this angle through **O** label the end of this line **E**. Now bisect the angle ∠EOB. Draw the line through **O** which bisects this angle. Label its end **F**.
Finally bisect the angle ∠AOC draw a line through **O** and label its end **G**.

1) Use your ruler to measure the lengths **AO** and **OB**

2) Use your protractor to measure angles ∠AOC and ∠COB

3) Measure angle ∠EOB

4) Measure angles ∠EOF and ∠FOB

5) Measure angle ∠GOE

The answers are on the next page.

Key Stage 3 Maths Explained - Volume 2 Geometry

Answers to Exercise 31 to 33

Your Drawing should look like this

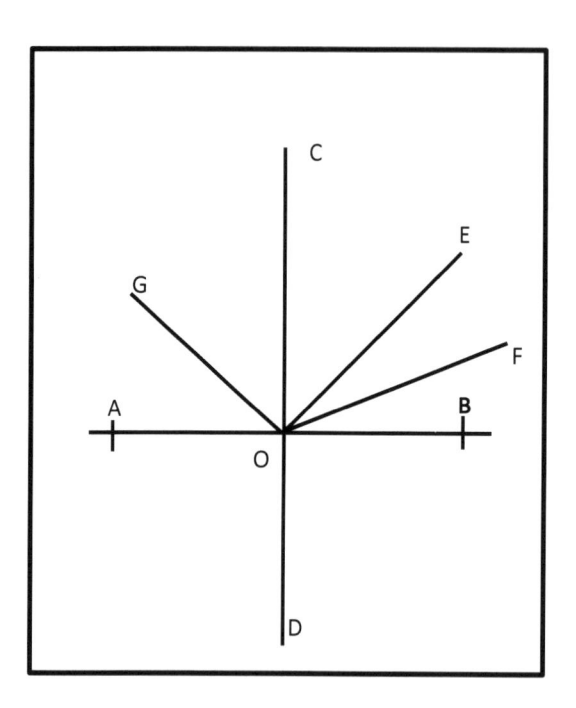

1) AO should be equal to OB when measured with your ruler.

2) ∠AOC and ∠COB should both be 90°.

3) Angle ∠EOB should be 45°.

4) Angles ∠EOF and ∠FOB should be between 22 and 23 degrees. (they are actually 22·5°)

5) Angle ∠GOE should be 90°

Chapter 34 – Triangles

A triangle is a closed shape with three sides, each of which is a straight line, drawn on a flat (or plane) surface.

A tip from your tutor: Maths is an exact and precise subject. So, you must define everything precisely, or you will get things wrong. You have been warned!

The **interior (inside) angles of a triangle add up to 180°**. This is true for all triangles so if are given 2 angles, you can find the third angle.

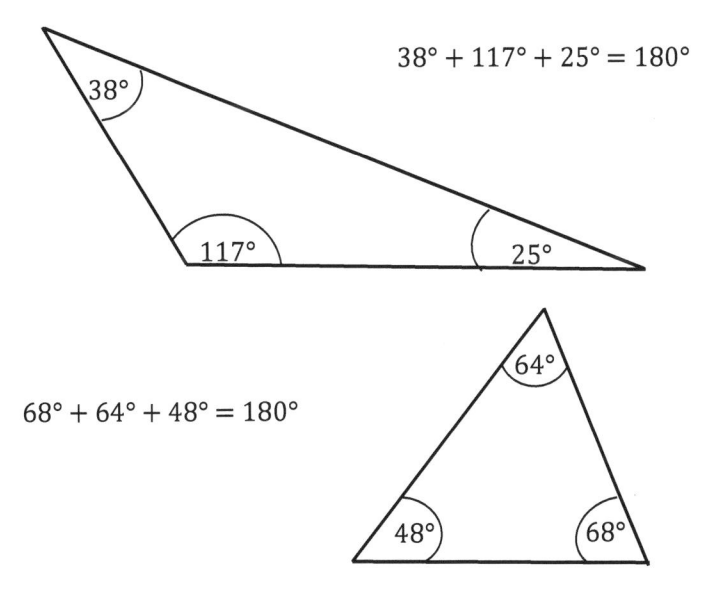

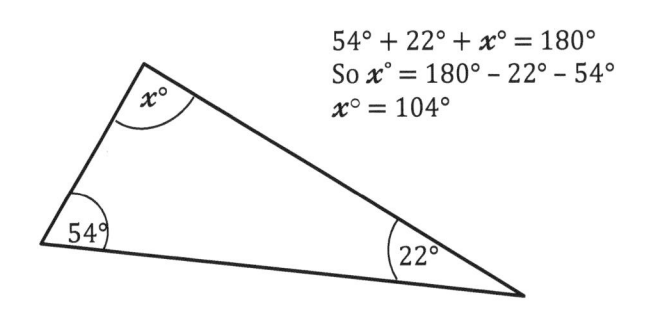

$38° + 117° + 25° = 180°$

$68° + 64° + 48° = 180°$

$54° + 22° + x° = 180°$
So $x° = 180° - 22° - 54°$
$x° = 104°$

Key Stage 3 Maths Explained - Volume 2 Geometry

There are five types of triangle:
scalene triangles,
isosceles triangles,
equilateral triangles,
right angled triangles
and obtuse angle triangles.

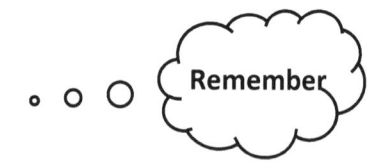

Remember

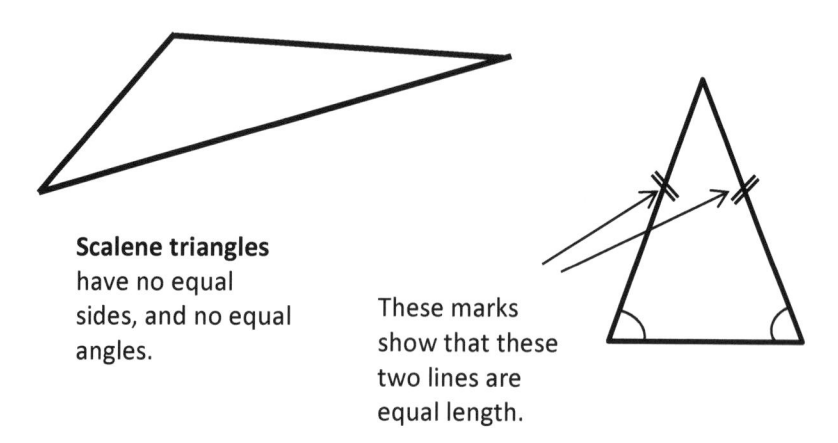

Scalene triangles have no equal sides, and no equal angles.

These marks show that these two lines are equal length.

Isosceles triangles have two equal sides and two equal angles. The three angles add up to 180°.

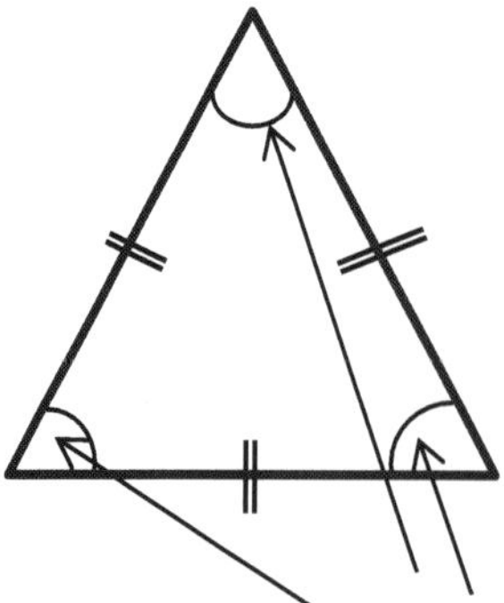

Equilateral Triangles have three equal sides and three equal angles. Angles add up to 180°, so each angle is 60°.

These arcs show that these three angles are equal

Chapter 34 – Triangles

A right-angle triangle has one angle which is 90⁰ (So, the other two angles must add up to 90⁰)

The side opposite the right angle is called the **hypotenuse "h"**

With respect to angle A, side **a** is known as the **opposite** side and side **b** is known as the **adjacent** side. The side **h** opposite to the right angle is called the **hypotenuse**

A square mark shows that this is a right angle

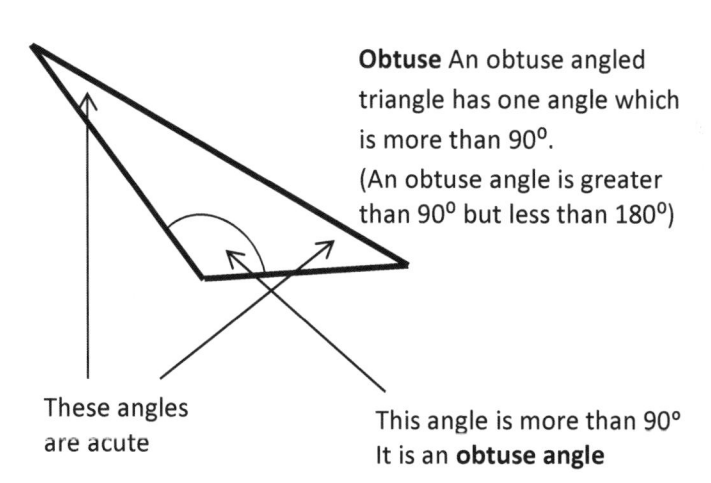

Obtuse An obtuse angled triangle has one angle which is more than 90⁰.
(An obtuse angle is greater than 90⁰ but less than 180⁰)

These angles are acute

This angle is more than 90°
It is an **obtuse angle**

Acute Angles are angles which are less than 90⁰

Remember

The three angles inside all triangles add up to 180⁰.

A tip from your tutor

'You need to know the names and shapes of these triangles. Put labeled diagrams where you will see them frequently. The names will be used in questions. If you don't know what they mean you won't be able to answer the questions! Make clear large drawings of these triangles – with their names – and put them somewhere where you will keep seeing them. Advertisers use this trick. They put up posters, inside and outside shops so that when you go in you remember the advertisement and buy their products. You can use it to help you with your maths! One of my pupils learned all of his formulae this way. He taped them to the vertical part of each step on the stairs. Two years later his younger brother knew them all – only he still had to find out what they meant! Use every method of learning that you can.'

Chapter 34 – Triangles

However easy this seems – and it is – do not forget it!

Look for triangles in more complicated diagrams and fill in as many angles as you can. It often helps to solve problems. Try this one;

Angle ∠ABC= 70°, Angle ∠ACB = 40°, find ∠BAC

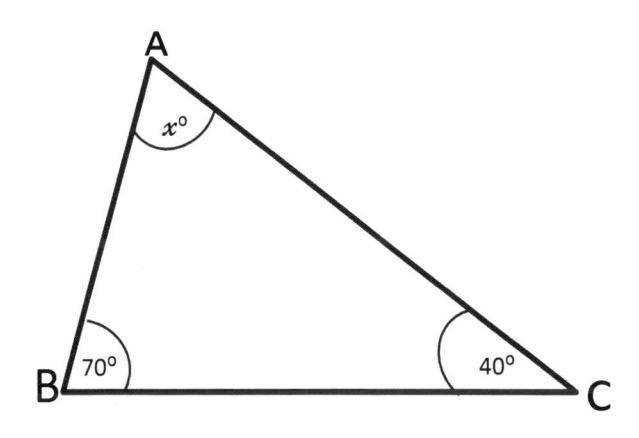

The sign ∠BAC shows that there is an angle at **A**. The letters BAC tells you that the line BA meets line AC at point A. So, in this diagram ∠ABC = 70°, and ∠ACB = 40°.

When you are naming angles you give them three letters.
The outside letters mark the ends of the two lines forming the angle.
So the angles in the triangle are ∠ABC = 70°, and ∠BCA = 40°, and ∠BAC = $x°$. (x means unknown).

As the angles must add up to 180°,
you can write 40° + 70° + $x°$ = 180°,
which makes $x°$ = 180° - 40° - 70° so ∠BAC = $x°$ = 70°.

Key Stage 3 Maths Explained - Volume 2 Geometry

Often you can get triangles with one side extended, giving an angle outside the triangle. (This is known as **an external angle**)
You are given the angles $\angle ABC$ and $\angle BAC$ and asked to find $\angle BCA$ and $\angle BCD$.

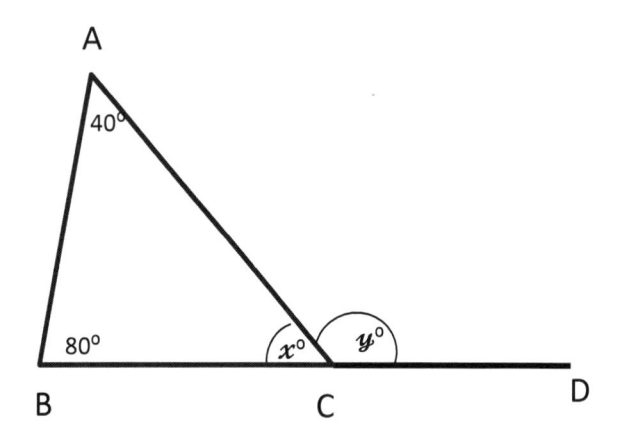

As the angles in a triangle add up to 180°, 70° + 40° + $x°$ = 180°
So $x°$ = 180° - 80° - 40°
$x°$ = 180° - 120° = 60°, so $\angle BCA$ = 60°

All angles on a straight line add up to 180°
$\angle BCD$ is a straight line so $\angle ACB$ + $\angle ACD$ = 180°
This means that 60° + $\angle ACD$ = 180°.
So y = $\angle BCD$ = 180° - 60° = 120°.
y = 120°.

From triangles you can learn how to look at many different geometric shapes, and how to think about geometry.

Chapter 34 – Triangles

Exercise 34

1) What type of triangle is this?

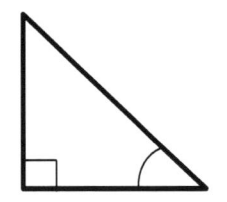

2) Label the hypotenuse 'h'
3) Label the sides of the triangle Which are opposite, 'o', and adjacent **a** to the marked angle.

4) What type of triangle is this?

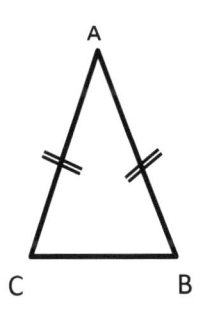

5) What do the two double lines mean?
6) What is important about the angles ∠ABC and ∠BCA?

7) What type of triangle is this?

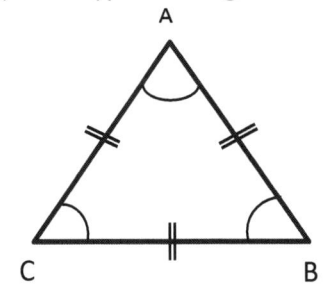

8) What are the size of the angles marked A, B, and C?
9) What is special about the lines AB, BC, and CA?

10) How is this triangle described?

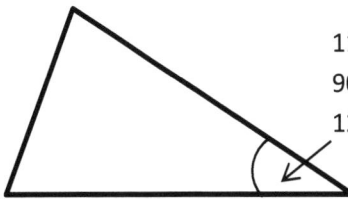

11) What is an angle bigger than 90° called?
12) How is this angle described?

Key Stage 3 Maths Explained - Volume 2 Geometry

Answers to Exercise 34

1) It is a right-angled triangle

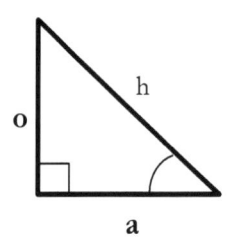

2) The hypotenuse is labeled **h**

3) **a** is adjacent to the marked angle
o is the side opposite to the marked angle

4) It is an isosceles triangle.

5) The marked sides are both the same length.

6) The marked angles are equal.

7) This is an equilateral triangle.

8) All three angles are equal with a value of 60°.

9) The three marked sides have the same length.

10) This is a scalene triangle (no equal angles or sides).

11) An angle greater than 90°is call an obtuse angle.

12) This angle is less than 90° and is "acute"

Chapter 35 – Similar Triangles

Draw a triangle: any triangle. Label the corners A,B,C (figure 1)
Extend the lines AB and CD well past the corners

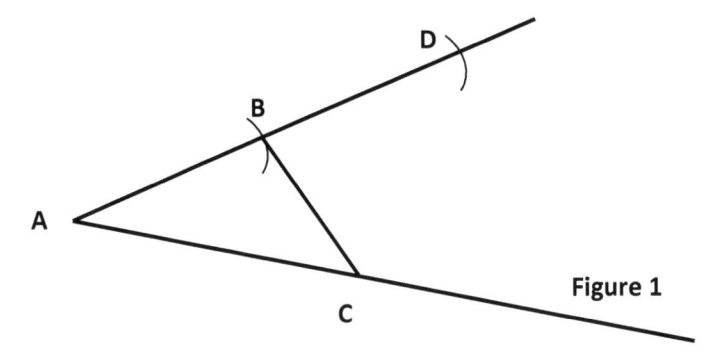

Figure 1

Now put the point of your pencil compasses on A and open them out to draw an arc at B. Now move the point to B without changing the angle and draw another arc at D. The length AD will be twice the length of AB.

Now do the same thing to the line **AC**
and mark another point **E**. (See figure 2)
Draw a line through **DE.**

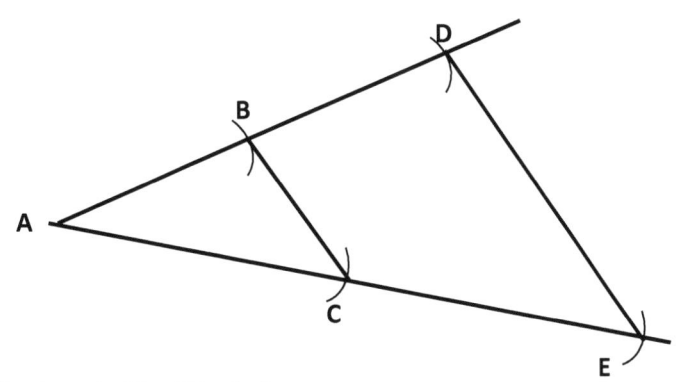

The length **AE** will be twice
the length AC, as shown in figure 2
Now put the point of your pencil compasses on **B**
and open them out to draw an arc through **C**, figure 3.

Figure 2

Key Stage 3 Maths Explained - Volume 2 Geometry

Move the point to D without changing the setting of the compass and draw an arc through DE Figure 3. Move the point to E and draw another arc.

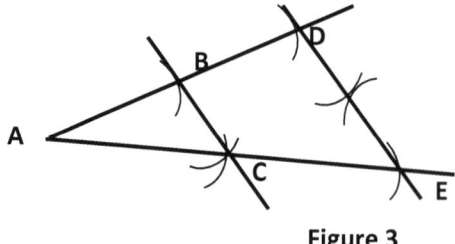

Figure 3

The two arcs should meet at the mid points of DE (Figure 3). You have constructed a pair of **Similar Triangles**, ABC and ADE. Line **DE** will be parallel to Line **CB**. The angle **∠ACB** is equal to the angle **∠AED**, and the angle **∠ABC** is equal to the angle **∠ADE**, and all the sides of **ADE** are twice the length of the sides of **ABC**.

The two triangles are **similar,** but not **Congruent Triangles** (they are not the same size). The sides of **ADE** are each twice as long as the sides of **ABC**, and the area of the larger triangle is 4 times the area of the smaller. The **scale** of the larger triangle is 2 times that of the smaller.

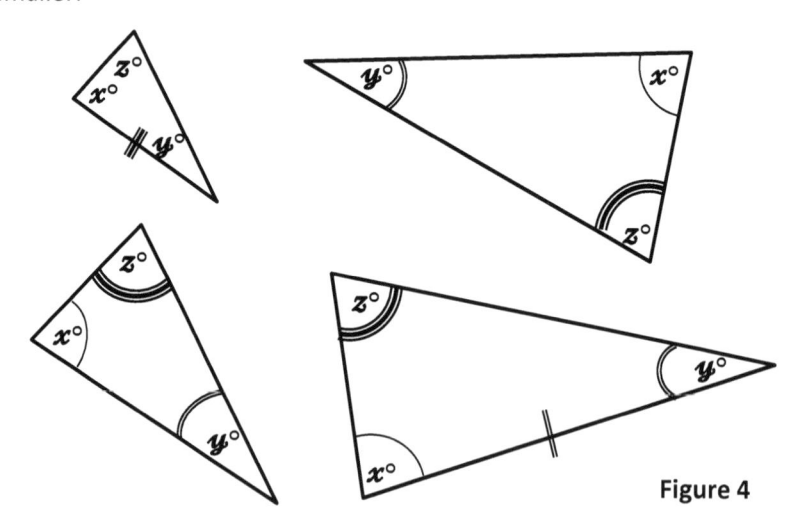

Figure 4

The four triangles (figure 4) are all similar. Their angles are identical. They have different sizes and have been rotated with respect to one another but have all been scaled from the same original drawing: they are **Similar Triangles**. Each of the triangles has the same angles.

Chapter 35 – Similar Triangles

If you know the size of two angles of a triangle ($x°$, and $y°$) you will know the size of the third angle $z°$, since for all triangles
$x° + y° + z° = 180°$.
So, all these triangles are similar, but are drawn to different scales. To find the size (or scale) of any triangle you need to know the length of the side between the two marked angles.

If you know that the side marked ‖ is twice as long as the side of the small triangle marked ∣∣∣ then you know that all the sides of the large triangle are twice the size of the similar side of the small triangle.

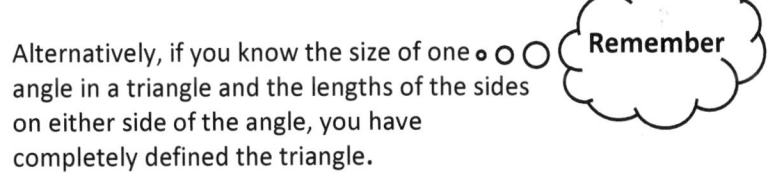

Remember

Alternatively, if you know the size of one angle in a triangle and the lengths of the sides on either side of the angle, you have completely defined the triangle.

Remember

If a pair of identical angles are the same in two triangles and the side between the angles are the same length the triangles are **congruent**
If two sides of a pair of triangles are have the same lengths and the angles between the sides are the same, then this pair of triangles is **congruent.** They may be twisted round but they are still congruent

The Use of Similar Triangles: Maps

An important uses of similar triangles is in drawing maps. You may find Ordnance Survey reference points on old buildings and on the tops of hills. **Reference points** need to have a clear view of other distant objects in several different directions. They often take the form of a stone pillar about a meter high with a brass plate on the top giving the name of the point

Modern Ordnance Survey maps are drawn to a scale of 50,000 to 1. That is 1 cm on the map corresponds to 50,000 cm = 0·5 km on the ground. (Older maps were drawn to a scale of 1 inch to the mile, a ratio of 63,360 to 1.) For very accurate purposes there are even larger scale maps. Road maps are usually produced to a scale of 4 miles to the inch, but they are based on the Ordnance Survey's original measurements.

Key Stage 3 Maths Explained - Volume 2 Geometry

Nowadays surveyors use digital range finders and very accurate angular scales, but the original very accurate maps were drawn over two hundred years ago using an optical instrument known as a **theodolite.**

These theodolites used built-in protractors, nearly a metre across. Their scales were engraved by a machine to make them very accurate. The theodolites were mounted on horizontal tables, kept level by a system of weights.

The theodolite is placed over one of the reference points. The angles are then measured between several prominent points in the landscape, such as church towers. The theodolite can then be moved to one of the identified points and a fresh set of angles measured. This is continued until the whole area is covered with a set of triangles.

A carefully measured distance is needed to scale the first few triangles. This is known as **the baseline.** Once this has been done, the first, and all subsequent triangles can be scaled to give the distances between the points identified on the ground.

The originally Ordnance Survey **base line** was created on Hounslow Heath. (a line which now crosses Heathrow airport) as this was the flattest suitable ground. The original base line was five miles long. Using theodolites and trigonometry; a network of accurately measured triangles was created all over Britain and eventually extended across the Straits of Dover to France and then back to a verification baseline in Kent.

Maps could then be drawn to show all the reference points used at the corners of triangles with identical angles but with the lengths of their sides reduced to match the scale of the map, which nowadays is 50,000 to 1.

Chapter 35 – Similar Triangles

Exercise 35

1) Triangles ① and ② are similar. What is their scale, and what is the length of the side marked x?

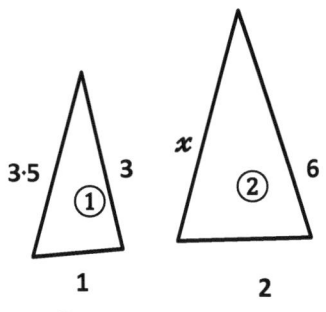

2) Are the right-angle triangles ③ and ④ similar?

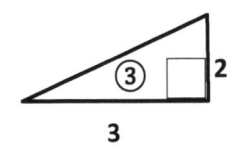

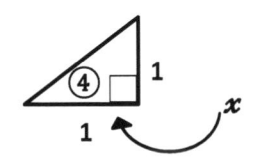

3) How big would side x have to be to make them similar?

4) What would the ratio of the sizes then be?

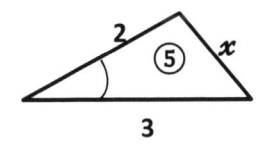

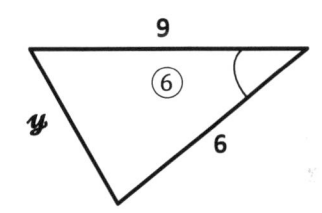

5) The angles marked on the two triangles ⑤ and ⑥ are the same. If $x = 1$ what is the sizes of y?

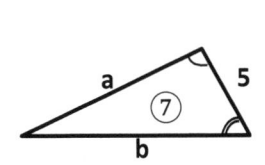

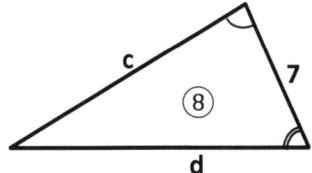

In the two triangles ⑦ and ⑧ the angles marked with a single curve are the same. Also, the angles marked with a double curve Are the same as one another.

a) Are these two triangles congruent or similar?

b) What is the ratio $\dfrac{c}{a}$, and   c) What is the ratio $\dfrac{d}{b}$?

Key Stage 3 Maths Explained - Volume 2 Geometry

Answers to Exercise 35

1) The lengths of the sides of triangle ② are twice those of triangle ①. So, side x must be $2 \times 3\cdot5 = 7$

2) In the two right angle triangles ③ and ④ the ratios of the vertical sides are $\frac{2}{1}$, but the ratios of the horizontal sides are $\frac{3}{1}$ so they are not similar.

3) To make the triangles into a pair of similar triangles the side marked x would have to be increased to 1·5.

4) Triangle ③ would then be twice the size of triangle ④.

5) The lengths of the sides marked on triangle ⑥ are twice the lengths of those on triangle ⑤. So $y = 2x$

6)
a) The two triangles ⑦ and ⑧ are similar, not congruent because they are of different sizes.

b) The ratio $\frac{c}{a}$, is $\frac{7}{5}$

c) The ratio $\frac{d}{b}$, is $\frac{7}{5}$

Chapter 36 – Quadrilaterals

Quadrilaterals have four straight sides; it doesn't matter what shape they are; it's the four straight sides that count.

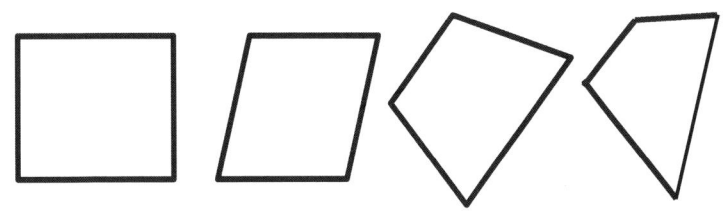

With all these shapes you can obviously draw a line from one corner to the opposite corner

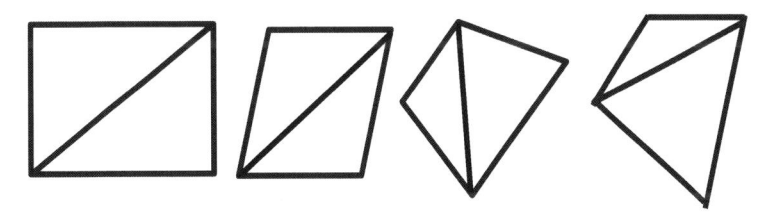

Equally obviously this divides the quadrilateral into two triangles. Each triangle has a total of 180° in its angles, so each quadilateral must have 2 × 180° = 360° as the total of its inside angles.

As you can see quadrilaterals can have many shapes. Geometry separates these shapes into groups which have similar properties.

A square has four equal sides and four equal angles. If you divide it into two you have two triangles. Each triangle has 180°, so the square has 360°. It is drawn so that all the angles are equal, so each angle is 90°.

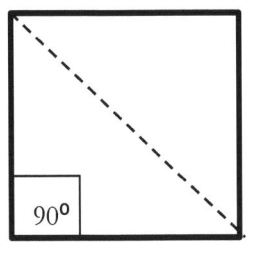

Key Stage 3 Maths Explained - Volume 2 Geometry

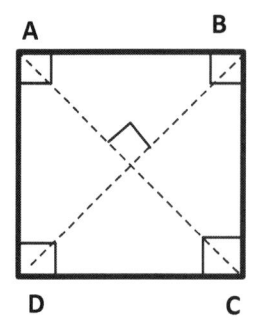

You can fold a square along either diagonal, and get the same sized triangle.
So the diagonals are equal.

This means that the diagonals must cross at 90°

If the square is pushed sideways it still has four equal sides but the angles have changed.

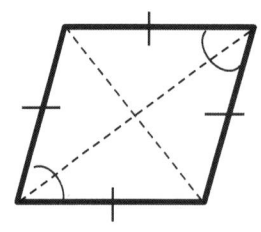

It is now a **rhombus.** The opposite angles are equal. The diagonals still cross at right angles but they are now of different lengths; one is longer than the other. The diagonals still cross at their mid points.

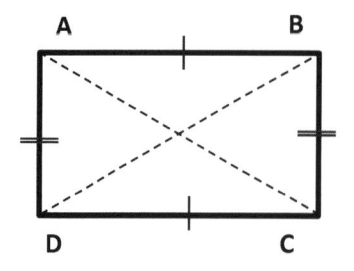

The **rectangle** has four right angles. It however has one pair of sides, (AB and CD) longer than the other pair (AD and BC). The diagonals are still the same length still cross at mid points; but NOT at right angles.

Chapter 36 – Quadrilaterals

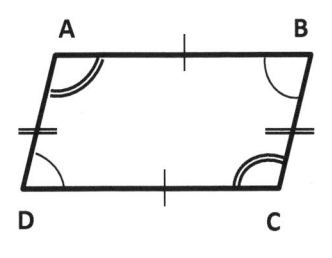

The **parallelogram** is like a rectangle pushed sideways. There are two pairs of equal sides.
(AB = CD) and (AD = CB)
AB and CD are parallel as are AD and BC. The **perimeter** of a parallelogram is **2(AB + BC)**

Parallel lines are like railway lines. However long they are, they always have to keep exactly the same distance apart, or the train would come off the rails!

In a parallelogram the opposite angles are equal:

$$\angle ADC = \angle ABC \quad \text{and} \quad \angle DAB = \angle BCD$$

The diagonals intersect each other (that is they cross at their mid points) but they are of different lengths.

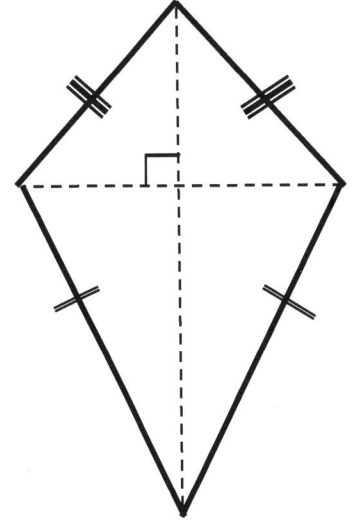

The **Kite** has two pairs of equal sides, but they are side by side not opposite. The diagonals cross at right angles. The longer diagonal bisects the kite – that is cuts it into two equal parts.

Key Stage 3 Maths Explained - Volume 2 Geometry

This is a **Trapezium**. It has one pair of parallel sides. If the other two sides are the same length then it is an **isosceles trapezium**.

In an **isosceles trapezium** the pair of angles marked with a single line is equal, as are the pair of angles marked with a double line

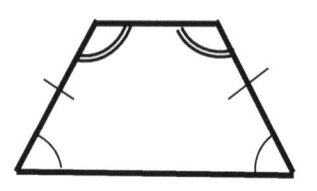

The other **trapezium** has one pair of parallel sides but has no other conditions. The sides are of different lengths, and the angles are different, though they still add up to 360°.

Remember these names, and their shapes
Square
Rhombus
Rectangle
Parallelogram
Kite
Trapezium
Isosceles Trapezium

Now that you know the shapes we can look at them in more detail in the next chapter.

Chapter 37 – Areas

This chapter looks at areas. An area measures flat space. Think of the floor of a room. If it is an empty room then you see how much floor there is (figure 1). The size of the floor is measured by finding how long it is and how wide it is.

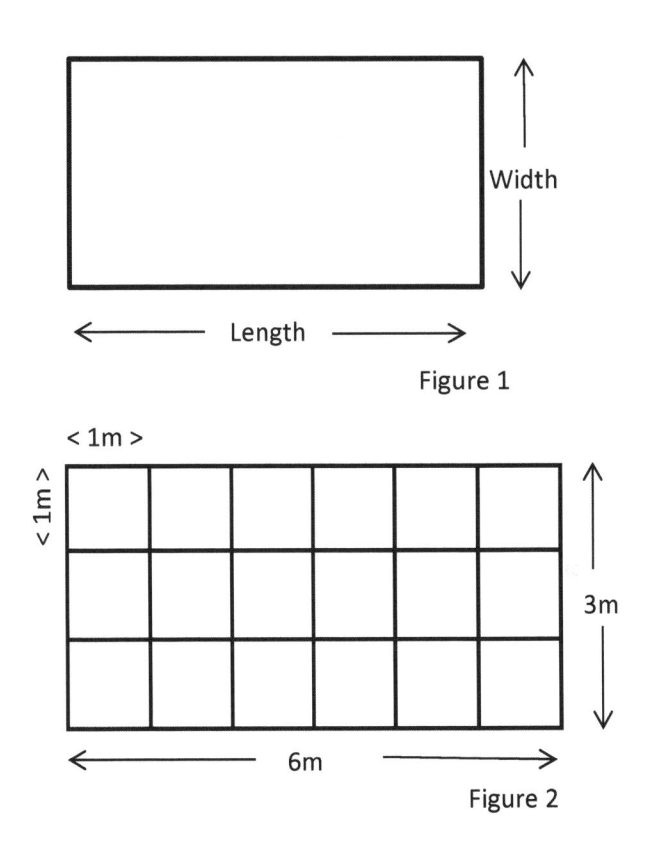

Figure 1

Figure 2

To measure the floor, you will find how long it is, say 6 meters, and how wide it is, say 3 meters. You could make chalk marks along the floor every 1m along the length, and every 1m across the width of the floor (figure 2).

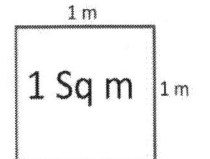

This makes squares which have sides 1m in length and the area is called 1 square meter (obviously). 1 square meter is the unit of measurement for an area.

159

Key Stage 3 Maths Explained - Volume 2 Geometry

That area could be a narrow strip of ribbon 1cm (0.01m) wide and 100m long, or a section of floor 1 m wide and 1 m long.

A tip from your tutor

Whatever the shape, the unit of measurement of an area is 1 square meter, usually written as 1sq m. A square meter can also be written metres² or m².
(The little 2 at the top means squared)
These are the units you must use.

'Lengths are easy to change, 100cm = 1m. If you wait till you have areas then 1m² = 10,000cm², and it's easy to make mistakes. When you get to volumes it will be worse! So, start now and avoid mistakes.

Now you can see from Figure 5 that if you have a square or a rectangle, then finding the area is simple. You measure the length and the width in meters (m) and that will give you the area in m². When you write the area make quite sure you put **m²**, or you have given a totally wrong answer.

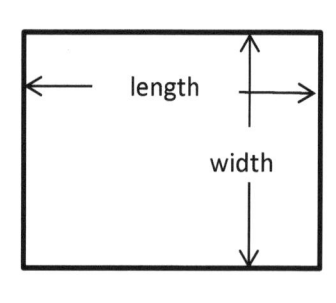

Figure 5

Chapter 37 – Areas

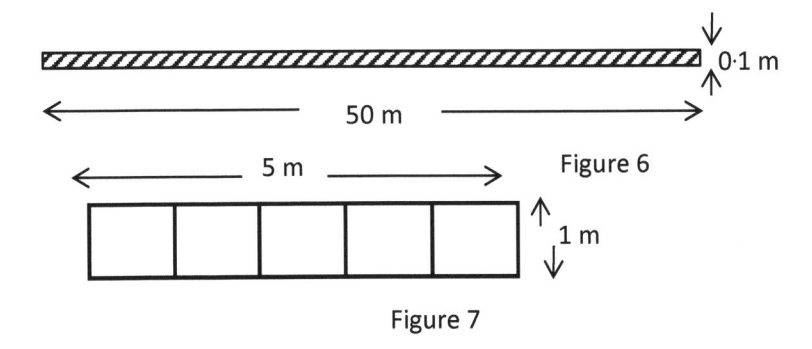

50 m, 0.1 m

Figure 6

5 m, 1 m

Figure 7

5m² is the area of a rectangle. Both the rope and the carpet have areas of one square m, but their lengths are very different.

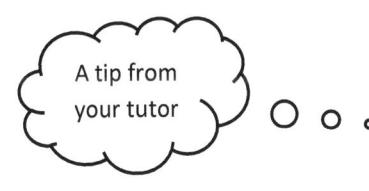

A tip from your tutor

A strong piece of rope gives practice for a tight rope walker.

An area of carpet in a front room gives a good place to sit when it's snowing outside. Don't confuse them!

Exercise 37

1) A carpet measures 3 meters by 2.5 meters.
a) What is its area?
b) If the carpet is sold at £15.00 per square meter, how much will it cost?

2) A patio paving tile measure 0·2 meters by 0·2 meters.
a) What is the area in square meters of each tile?
b) A patio measures 4 meters by 2 meters. What is its area?
c) How many tiles will be needed to cover the patio?

3) A paving slabs measure 0·66 meters square, that is 0·66m × 0·66m.
a) What is its area?
b) A yard measures 12 meters by 15 meters what is its area?
c) How many slabs will it take to pave it?

4) A ribbon is 3cm wide and 50 meters long. What is its area in square meters?

Key Stage 3 Maths Explained - Volume 2 Geometry

Answers to Exercise 37

1)   a) The area of the carpet is 7·5 m²
    b) At £15·00 per m² the carpet would cost £ 112·50

2)
    a) The area of each tile is 0·2 × 0·2 = 0·04 m²
    b) The area of the patio is 4 × 2 = 8m²
    c) The number of tiles needed to pave it is
    $8 \div 0·04 = \dfrac{8}{0·04} = 200$ tiles

3)
    a) The area of each slab is 0·66 × 0·66 = 0·4356 m²
    b) The area of the yard is 12 meters by 15 meters = 180 m²
    c) The number of slabs needed is $\dfrac{180}{0·4356} = 413$

4) To find he area of the ribbon in m² we must convert its width into meters 3cm = $\dfrac{3}{100}$ = 0·03m   So the area is 50 × 0·03 = 1·5m²

Chapter 38 - Areas of Triangles

This chapter shows you how to find the **Area of Triangles**.
In chapter 37 we found the areas of squares and rectangles. Triangles are just as easy – they are, after all parts of rectangles.
Look at Figure 1.

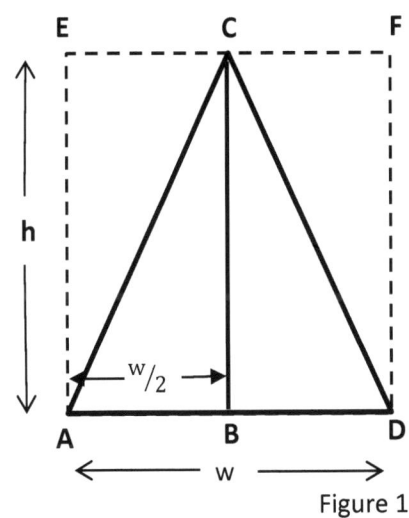

The triangle (ABC) has been enclosed by a rectangle (dotted lines). The rectangle is the same height as the triangle.
The **base of the triangle** is AB which is also one side of the rectangle. D is the middle of AB. EF is the top of the rectangle; C is the middle of EF.

Figure 1

There are two rectangles in the diagram, AECD and BFCD. The line CA and CB are diagonals of the rectangle and so cut the rectangles in half.

The area of AECD is $h \times \dfrac{w}{2} = \dfrac{hw}{2}$.

The area of $\dfrac{1}{2}$ the triangle (ABC) is half the area of AECD = $\dfrac{hw}{4}$. The rectangle BFCD has an area of $h \times \dfrac{w}{2} = \dfrac{hw}{2}$.

So, ADC has an area of $\dfrac{1}{2} \times \dfrac{hw}{2} = \dfrac{hw}{4}$.

In the same way you can find the area of BFCD ($\frac{w}{2} \times h = \frac{hw}{2}$).
CB cuts this rectangle in half.

So, the triangle BCD has an area of $\frac{1}{2} \times \frac{hw}{2} = \frac{hw}{4}$.

The area of the triangle ABC = $\frac{1}{2}$ area of AECD + $\frac{1}{2}$ area of BFCD

$$= \frac{hw}{4} + \frac{hw}{4} = \frac{2hw}{4} = \frac{hw}{2} = h \times \frac{w}{2}.$$

This is $\frac{1}{2} \times w \times h = \frac{1}{2}$ width × height.

So, the area of a triangle is $\frac{1}{2}$ × width × height.

You can draw rectangles like this around any triangle and get the same result. You may have to turn some of the triangles round first, like the one in Figure 2

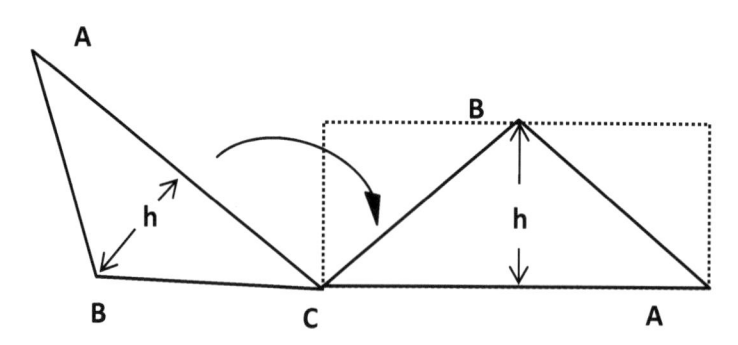

Figure 2

Again, the area is half the width times the height $\frac{1}{2}$ CA × h

164

Chapter 38 - Areas of Triangles

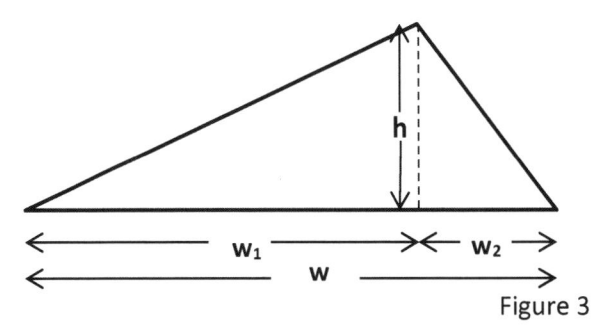

In figure 3 the triangle is not isosceles; the two halves are different. The area is ½ h × w_1 + ½ h × w_2 = ½ h × (w_1 + w_2) = ½ h × w which again is: half the width times the height

Exercise 38

Calculate the areas of the following triangles. Include the units.

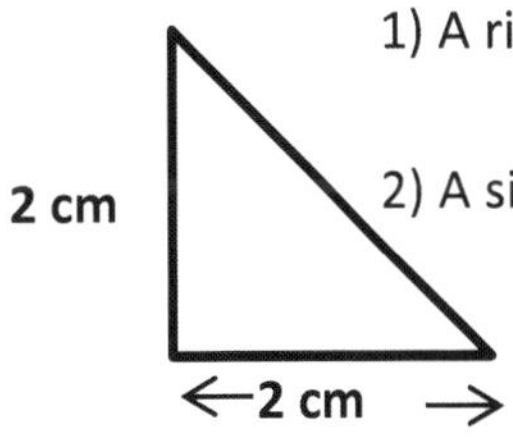

1) A right-angle triangle, 2cm wide and 2cm high.

2) A similar triangle 4cm wide and 4cm high.

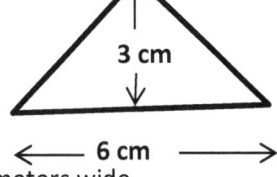

3) An equiangular triangle 3 cm high and 6 cm wide.

4) A scalene triangle 5 meters high and 7 meters wide.

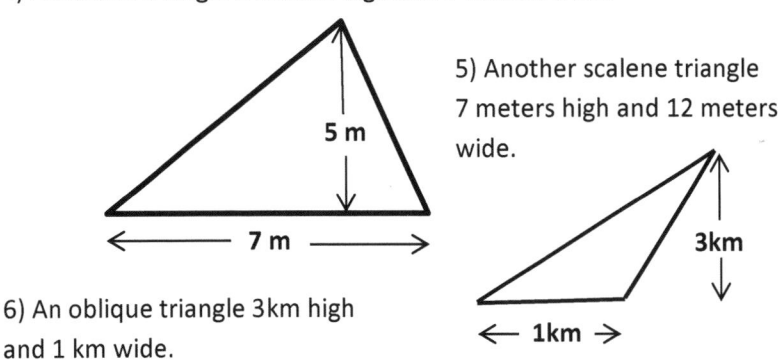

5) Another scalene triangle 7 meters high and 12 meters wide.

6) An oblique triangle 3km high and 1 km wide.

7) Another oblique triangle 5cm high and 2 cm wide.

Key Stage 3 Maths Explained - Volume 2 Geometry

Answers to Exercise 38

1) ½ × 2 × 2 = 2 cm²

2) ½ × 4 × 4 = 8 cm²

3) ½ × 3 × 6 = 9 cm²

4) ½ × 5 × 7 = 17·5 cm² (or 17½ cm²)

5) ½ × 5 × 12 = 30 m²

6) ½ × 1 × 3 = 1·5 km²

7) ½ × 5 × 2 = 5 cm²

Chapter 39 - Perimeters and Areas

Perimeters and Areas of Rectangles.

A perimeter is "all the way round the edge". A perimeter fence is a fence that goes all the way round the edge of a piece of land. It may be there to keep animals in. if a handful of cows got out of a field and wondered onto a motorway you can just imagine the confusion! So, there is a fence round the outside edge, or perimeter, of the field to stop the cows getting out. The length of the fence is the length of the perimeter.

If you have a square then it's easy to find the perimeter
If the side of the square is ℓ then the perimeter is obviously

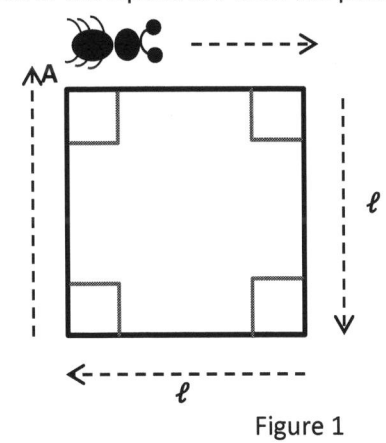

$\ell + \ell + \ell + \ell$

To help you to work this out I have an imaginary "perimeter ant" which starts at one corner, A, of a diagram (Figure 1) and runs all the way round the edge till it gets back to A again (this is a helpful idea – but don't boast about it!).

Figure 1

So, **perimeters** are simply the "distance round the edge".

If you look at a rectangle, (figure 2) the distance round the edge will be

$\ell + w + \ell + w$ which is
$2(\ell + 2w)$

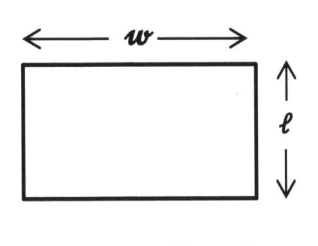

Figure 2

167

Key Stage 3 Maths Explained - Volume 2 Geometry

If the rectangle is pushed sideways to make a **parallelogram**, its perimeter is just the same (2ℓ + 2w)
Nice to have something easy for once!

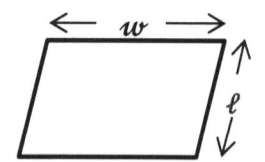

You must read the questions carefully when it comes to a mixture of shapes. There are questions that deal with several shapes. There are never too many in one question. You could have the one in figure 3 and be asked to find both the area of the shape and its perimeter.

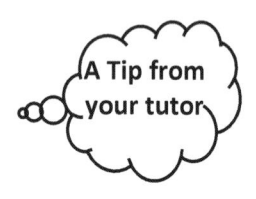

A Tip from your tutor

This Area is ABGJ and CDEF and a triangle GHJ. You are asked to find the area of the shape.

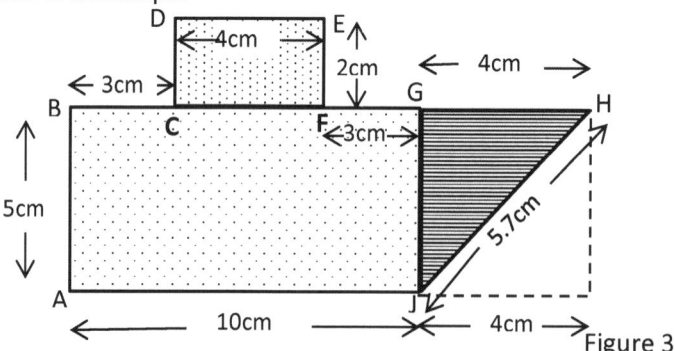

Figure 3

If you look at this carefully you have a large rectangle ABGJ, a small rectangle CDEF, and a triangle GHJ. You are asked to find the area of the shape.

The area is another rectangle ABGJ, shaded

There is another rectangle CDEF shaded

There is a triangle GHJ, shaded

First work out the areas, Take them separately.
1) ABGJ, this is a rectangle 5cm (AB) by 10cm (AJ)

Chapter 39 - Perimeters and Areas

So, its area is 5cm × 10cm area = 50cm².

2) CDEF, this is another rectangle 4cm (DE) by 2cm (EF) area = 8cm²

3) GJH, this is a triangle which is half a rectangle. The rectangle is 5cm × 4cm. The area of the rectangle is 5 × 4 = 20cm². So, half the area is 20 ÷ 2 = 10cm².

The whole area is 50cm² (ABGJ) + 8cm² (CDEF) + 10cm² (GHJ)

    50 + 8 + 10 = 68

    So, the area is **68cm²**.

'Now to work out the perimeter. You find this by adding the lengths of all the outside sides (remember the perimeter ant).'

A → B = 5cm
B → C = 3cm
C → D = 2cm
D → E = 4cm
E → F = 2cm
F → G = 3cm
G → H = 4cm
H → J = 5.7cm
J → A = <u>10cm</u>
Total = <u>38.7cm</u>

So, the perimeter is **38.7 cm**

Key Stage 3 Maths Explained - Volume 2 Geometry

Here is another problem. Find the area of this shape.

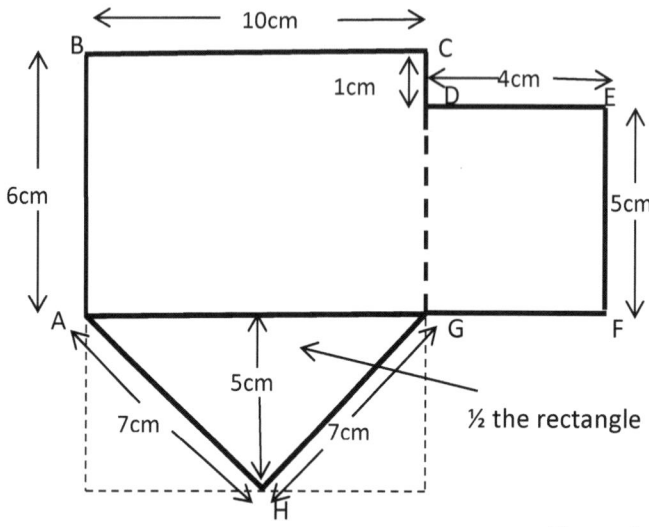

Figure 4

There are 3 parts ABCG, DEFG, and AGH.

ABCD is a rectangle 6cm × 10cm = 60cm²,
DEFG is a rectangle 4cm × 5cm = 20 cm²,
AGH is a triangle – the height is 5cm, the base is 10cm,
so, area = **½ base × height** = $\frac{1}{2}$ × 10 × 5 = 5 × 5 = 25cm².

The whole area is then 60 + 20 + 25 = **105cm²**.
The perimeter is (starting at A) 6 + 10 + 1 + 4 + 5 + 4 + 7 + 7 = **44cm.**
AB, BC, CD, DE, EF, FG, GH, HA

To help you be quite sure you have them all there, then count them all. Count the different areas – count your calculations. The letters describing the areas are in alphabetical order, so if you go around starting with **A** and ending with **A** you will have included everything.

Chapter 39 - Perimeters and Areas

Exercise 39

1) A swimming pool measures 15m by 30m, and is surrounded by a paved area 5m wide.
a) What is the perimeter of the pool?
b) What is the area of the pavement?
c) How many square tiles measuring 0·25 m by 0·25 are needed to pave it?

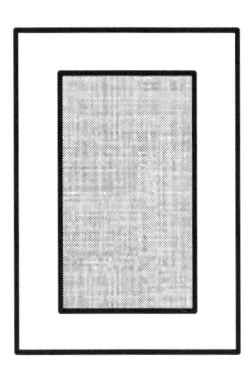

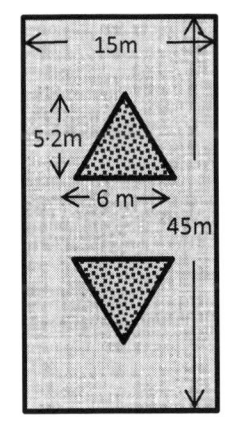

2) A lawn measuring 45m by 15m is to be turfed, except for two identical flower beds in the form of equilateral triangles 6m wide and 5·2m high.
a) What is the perimeter of each flower bed?
b) What is the area to be turfed?
c) Turf is delivered in pieces 30cm by 90cm, what is the smallest number of pieces needed?

3) The central square in this figure measures 12cm on each side. The height of each triangle is also 12cm, so the length of each outer side is 13·4m.
a) What is the perimeter of the figure?
b) What is its area?

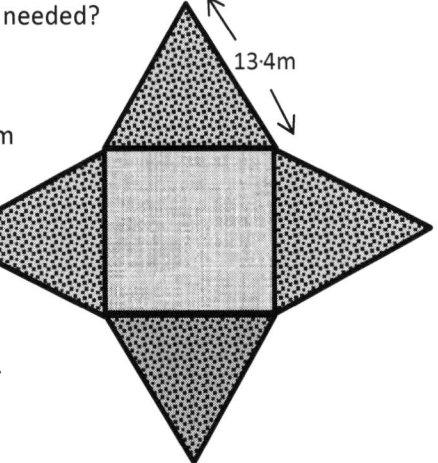

Key Stage 3 Maths Explained - Volume 2 Geometry

Answers to Exercise 39

1) a) The perimeter of the pool is 2(15 + 30) = 90m
   b) The total width of the bath plus pavement is 15 + 5 + 5 m = 25m.
   Its total length is 30 + 5 + 5 = 40m.
   So, its area is 25 × 40 = 1000m².

A tip from your Tutor

It is safer to subtract one area from another Than to try to work out the area of the 5 m wide pavement.

The area of the bath is 15 × 30 = 450m².
So, the paved area is 1000 − 450 = 550m²

c) The area of the tiles is 0·25 × 0·25 = 0·0625m².
The number of tiles needed is $\frac{550}{0·0625}$ = 8800 tiles

2) a) The perimeter of each triangular flower bed is
   6 + 6 + 6 = 18m
   b) The area of the lawn before subtracting the flower beds is
   15 × 45 = 675m². Each flower bed has an area of
   (½ base × height) = ½ × 5·2 × 6 = 15·6m²
   The area to be turfed is 675 − 2 × 15·6 = 643.8m²
   c) The area of 1 piece of turf is 30cm by 90cm
   which is 0·3 × 0·9 m = 0·27m²
   So, you will need $\frac{643·8}{0·27}$ = 2385 pieces of turf.
   (Note. The calculation gives 2384·444, but you can't buy less than one piece of turf!)

3) a) The perimeter of the figure is 8 × 13·4m = 107·2m
   b) The area of the figure is the area of the square plus four triangles. Area = 12 × 12 + 4 × ½ × 12 × 12 = 144 + 288 = 432c

Chapter 40 - Right Angle Triangles, Pythagoras

The right-angled triangle is a triangle in which one angle is 90°. Right angles are extremely important. Almost all buildings are designed with walls that are at right angles to the floor, and with right angled corners. Use some other shape and everything in the building will have to be made specially: and that is horribly expensive.

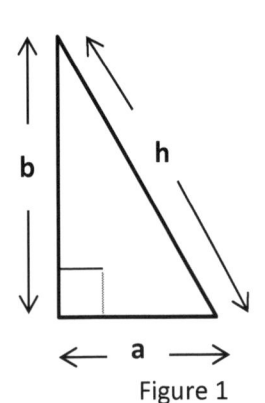

Furniture, plumbing and electrical fittings, doors and windows are all designed with right angled corners. Not only would any other angle be very expensive but anyone living in such a building would feel very unhappy: it would look wrong and leave them feeling a bit sick.

Figure 1

Over 2000 years ago a Greek philosopher called Euclid wrote a book in which he included a theorem by **Pythagoras.** This showed that if you know the length of any two sides of a right-angled triangle you can work out the length of the third side. He proved that this would always be true for triangles of any size or shape provided one angle was 90°

The side opposite the right angle is called the **hypotenuse.** In Figure 1 its length is shown as **h**. The lengths of the other two sides are marked **a** and **b**.

The Pythagoras theorem says that for any right-angled triangle
$h^2 = a^2 + b^2$.
So, if **a = 3**, and **b = 4** then
$h^2 = 3 \times 3 + 4 \times 4 = 9 + 16 = 25$ So $h = \sqrt{25} = 5$

Another right-angled triangle with whole number solutions has sides a and b which are 12 and 5 then $h^2 = 12^2 + 5^2 = 144 + 25 = 169$.
So, $h^2 = \sqrt{169} = 13$

Key Stage 3 Maths Explained - Volume 2 Geometry

This theorem is used in practice in all sorts of ways. Suppose you have to lay out the positions for the walls of a new building. You have a surveyor's tape measure a mallet and a bundle of stakes. First you knock in two stakes, 30 meters apart, close to the edge of the road, at A and B. (Figure 2)

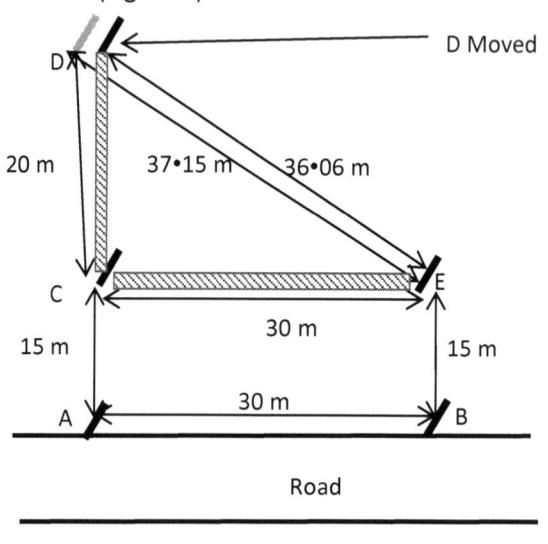

```
           D                              D Moved

  20 m         37·15 m      36·06 m

         C
                     30 m
   15 m                             15 m
                     30 m
         A                             B

                    Road
```

Figure 2

The plans tell you to measure 15 meters back from the edge of the road; so, you do this, and hammer in another stake at C. Then you measure 20 meters back from the first post and hammer in a third stake D. Go back to C and measure the width for the new building which is to be 30 meters wide. Before hammering in stake E, you move the end of the tape measure round in an arc until it is 15 meters from the road, and at right angles to it. Hammer in stake E. Now here comes the crucial bit. (This is where Pythagoras comes in.) Measure the diagonal from D to E. It is 37·15 meters. Is that right? Get out you calculator and work out
$20^2 + 30^2 = 400 + 900 = 1300$ meters squared.
Find the square root of 1300. $\sqrt{1300} = 36·055$ meters.
But you measured the diagonal as 37·15
This is 37·15 − 36·06 = 1·11 meters too big.

Chapter 40 - Right Angle Triangles, Pythagoras

The angle ∠ECD must be more than 90°. So, you will have to pull stake D out and move it about a meter to the right and try again. You may have to repeat this more than once until the diagonal measures 36·06. When this is right, you can go on and layout the rest of the building. It is very much better to spend time getting all the angles right, than to have to pull down and rebuild walls! Or even redraw a diagram!

You can also use the **Pythagoras formula** to find the third side of a right-angled triangle if you know the lengths of the hypotenuse and the length of one other side.
$b^2 = h^2 - a^2$ and $a^2 = h^2 - b^2$.
If $h = 5m$ and $b = 3m$ then $a^2 = h^2 - b^2$ gives $a^2 = 5 \times 5 - 3 \times 3$
So $a^2 = 25 - 9 = 16$, and $a = \sqrt{16} = 4$

Once away from Maths lessons some people have been known to try and apply "Pythagoras" to any three-cornered figure, with disastrous results. It only works with RIGHT ANGLED TRIANGLES on a PLANE (that is a flat) surface.

Warning

Exercise 40 (give your answers to two decimal places)

1) The hypotenuse of a right-angled triangle is 10 meters. What is the height of the triangle if its base is:
a) 2m, b) 3m, c) 3.5m, d) 5m, or e) 6m

2) A new lawn measures 5·5m by 3·5m. What is the length of the diagonal (hypotenuse)?

3) A 3m wide piece of carpet measures 6m across its diagonal (hypotenuse). How long is it?

4) How long is the hypotenuse of a right-angled triangle whose sides measured in meters are:
a) 8, 12   b) 26, 10   c) 1·41, 1·41   d) 1, 1·73

Key Stage 3 Maths Explained - Volume 2 Geometry

Answers to Exercise 40

1) a) 9•80m   b) 9•54m   c) 9•37m   d) 8•66m   e) 8m

2) 6•52m don't forget to add the m (meters).

3) 5•20m

4) a) 14•42m   b) 27•86m   c) 2•00m   d) 2•00m

Chapter 41 - Areas and Perimeters of Circles

Areas and perimeters of circles make use of a number which is represented by the Greek letter π pronounced Pi

Pi (π) is an infinitely long number, it is 3·141592654 to 9 decimal places. Someone worked it out to 200 decimal places, and more! You will only need to use 3·14 or the fraction $\frac{22}{7}$. An exam paper will tell you (either on the front cover or in the question) which value to use.

Back to the circle, the **radius** of a circle (goes from the center of a circle to the edge) it's called (r). The **diameter** (goes from the one side of a circle to the other and must pass through **the center**) It is called (d).

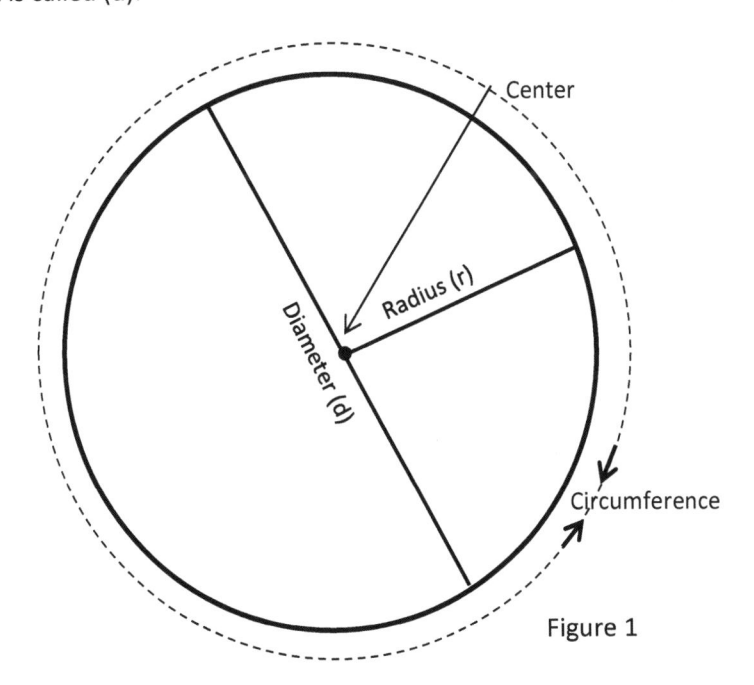

Figure 1

The distance all-round the edge of the circle (its perimeter) is called the **circumference** (c).
(It can also be called the **perimeter** of the circle.)

Key Stage 3 Maths Explained - Volume 2 Geometry

Radius, diameter, and circumference. You will need to know all these names as they will be used in questions. If you don't know them you will spend a lot of time looking them up! You do need to be able to use them. So here are some worked examples.

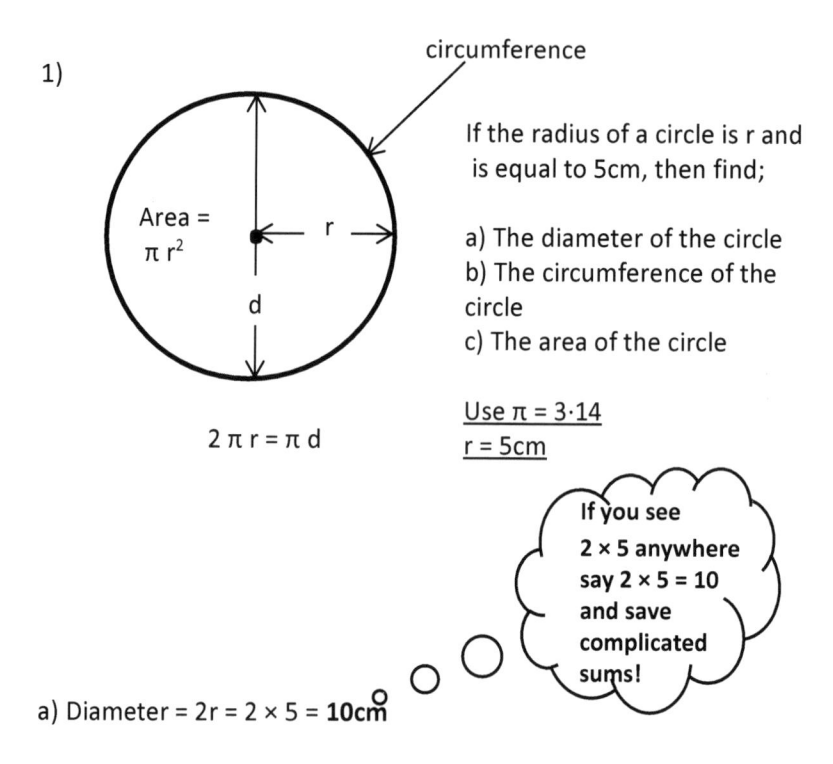

1)

Area = πr^2

$2\pi r = \pi d$

circumference

If the radius of a circle is r and is equal to 5cm, then find;

a) The diameter of the circle
b) The circumference of the circle
c) The area of the circle

Use $\pi = 3.14$
r = 5cm

If you see 2 × 5 anywhere say 2 × 5 = 10 and save complicated sums!

a) Diameter = 2r = 2 × 5 = **10cm**

b) Circumference = $2\pi r$ = 2 × 3·14 × 5cm
    = 2 × 5 × 3·14cm
    = 10 × 3·14cm
    = **31·4cm**

c) **Area = πr^2** = 3·14 × 5 × 5 = 3·14 × 25cm²
    = **78·5cm²**

178

Chapter 41 - Areas and Perimeters of Circles

For an area the unit is cm².

1cm² = area of square with sides of 1cm.

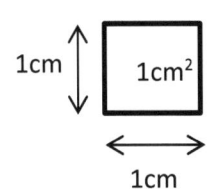

2) 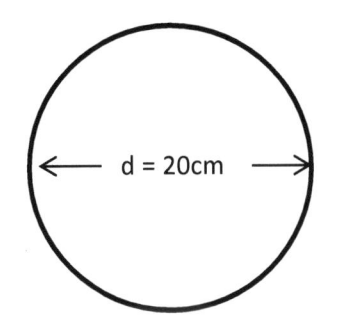 Find the radius, circumference and area of a circle where the diameter is 20cm.
Use π = 3·14

d = 20cm

a) **Diameter** = 20cm = 2 × radius
so, 2 × radius = 20
radius = $\frac{20}{2}$ = **10cm**

b) **Circumference** = 2 × π × r
= 2 × 3·14 × 10
= 2 × 31·4
= **62·8cm**

c) **Area** = π r² = π × 10 × 10
= 100 × 3·14
= **314cm²**

3) If the circumference is 50cm find the radius, the diameter and the area.
Use π = $\frac{22}{7}$

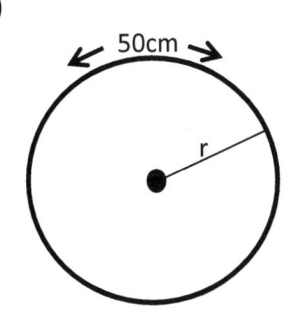

50cm

Diameter = 2r = 2 × 7·95
= **15·90**

Key Stage 3 Maths Explained - Volume 2 Geometry

Circumference = $2\pi r$ = 50

$$r = \frac{50}{2\pi} = \frac{50}{2 \times \frac{22}{7}} = \frac{50}{\frac{44}{7}}$$

$$r = \cancel{50}^{25} \times \frac{7}{\cancel{44}_{22}} = \frac{175}{22}$$

r = **7·95cm**

Area = πr^2 = 3·14 × 7·95 × 7·95
= **198·56cm²**

4) Area = 150cm²

The area of the circle is 150cm². Find the diameter and circumference.

Area = πr^2 = 150cm²   Circumference = $2\pi r$
$r^2 = \frac{150}{3\cdot 14} = 47\cdot 77$ = $2 \times \frac{22}{7} \times 6\cdot 91$
$r^2 = \sqrt{47\cdot 77}$ = **43·43cm**
   = **6·91cm**

Diameter = 2r = **13·82cm**

These are the only types of questions you may be set!

Chapter 41 - Areas and Perimeters of Circles

To find the center of a circle

Chapter 30 showed you how to use your pencil compasses to find the center of a line and to construct a right angle.

You can also use your pencil compasses to find the center of a circle. First open your compasses until the space between the points is a little more than the radius of the circle. It does not have to be exact. Stick the spike of the compasses somewhere on the circumference of the circle (marked ×) and draw an arc. Without changing the distance between the spike and the pencil, move the spike to a new point which is roughly $\frac{1}{3}$ of the way round the circle and draw a second arc. Do this again and draw a third arc. The center of the circle is inside the three arcs. To make this more accurate close the compasses a little until the three arcs just cross. They will cross at the center.

Exercise 41

Find the circumference and areas of the following circles.
(Don't forget the units) Use $\pi = 3 \cdot 14 = \frac{22}{7}$
Radius is: 1) 3cm, 2) 5km, 3) 2·2miles, 4) 17mm, 5) 3·72m
Diameter is: 6) 4·56m, 7) 18·2mm, 8) 92m, 9) 51km, 10) 5miles

Find the areas and radii of circles with these circumferences:
11) 32cm, 12) 55mm, 13) 150km, 14) 111m, 15) 2miles 16) 20cm

Key Stage 3 Maths Explained - Volume 2 Geometry

Answers to Exercise 41

1) The circumference of the circle is 18·849cm, its area is 28·278cm^2

2) The circumference of the circle is 31·42km, its area is 78·55km^2

3) The circumference of the circle is 13·825 miles, area, 15·207miles^2

4) The circumference of the circle is 106·828mm, area, 908·038mm^2

5) The circumference of the circle is 23·376m, its area is 43·480m^2

6) The circumference of the circle is 14·328 its area is 16·333m^2

7) The circumference of the circle is 57·184 its area is 260·189m^2

8) The circumference of the circle is 289·064m its area is 6648·472m^2

9) The circumference of the circle is 160·242km, area 2043·086km^2

10) The circumference of the circle is 15·71miles area, 19·6375miles^2

11) The area of the circle is 81·477cm^2, its radius is 5·092 cm

12) The area of the circle is 240·691mm^2, its radius is 8·752mm

13) The area of the circle is 1790·261km^2, its radius is 23·870km

14) The area of the circle is 980·350m^2, its radius is 17·664m

15) The area of the circle is 0·318miles^2, its radius is 0·318miles

16) The area of the circle is 31·827cm^2, its radius is 5·092 cm

Chapter 42 - Areas and Perimeters of Shapes

Areas and Perimeters of Shapes. This looks difficult, but all you need to do is keep track of what you are doing. The easiest way is to number all the bits clearly. Drawing circles round the numbers will help. Then calculate the values.

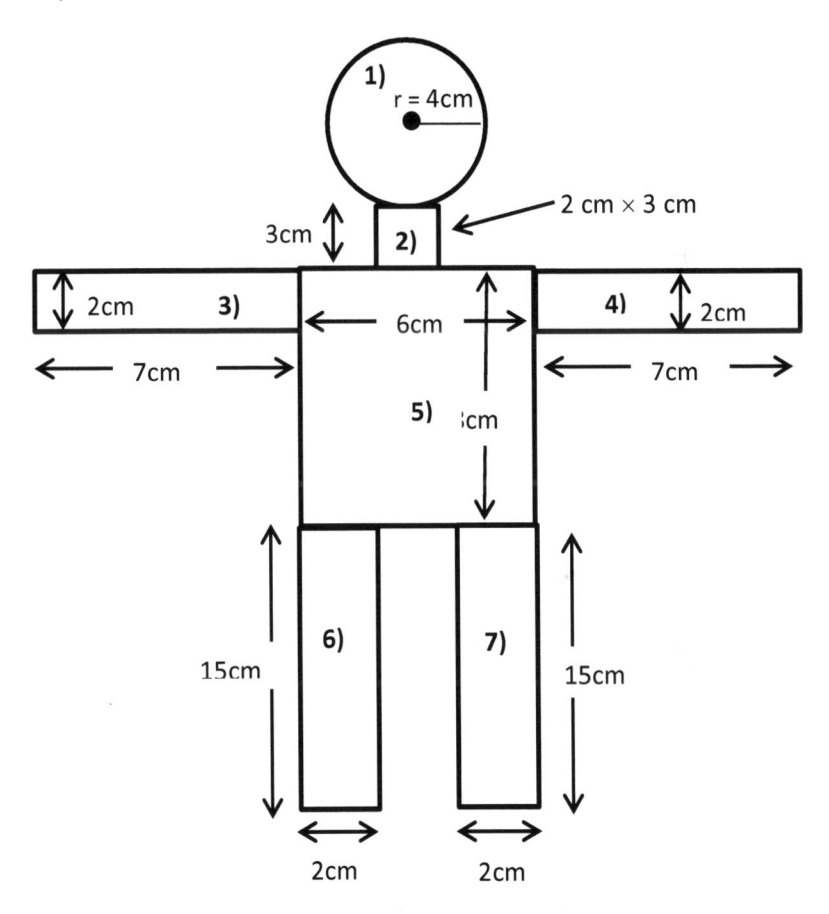

- 1) r = 4cm
- 2) 2 cm × 3 cm
- 3) 2cm, 7cm
- 4) 2cm, 7cm
- 5) 6cm, ;cm
- 3cm
- 6) 15cm, 2cm
- 7) 15cm, 2cm

Right away you have a complicated question. It breaks down into a set of very simple parts. Always look out for ways of doing questions step by step. Set out your work so that it is easy to see what you have done and check the answers.

Key Stage 3 Maths Explained - Volume 2 Geometry

Head	1) Circle r = 4cm. Area = π r² = π × 4 × 4 = **16πcm²**
Neck	2) Rectangle 3cm by 2cm = 3 × 2 = **6cm²**
Left arm	3) Rectangle 7cm by 2cm = 7 × 2 = **14cm²**
Right arm	4) Rectangle 7cm by 2cm = 7 × 2 = **14cm²**
Body	5) Rectangle 6cm by 8cm = 6 × 8 = **48cm²**
Left leg	6) Rectangle 15cm by 2cm = 15 × 2 = **30cm²**
Right leg	7) Rectangle 15cm by 2cm = 15 × 2 = **30cm²**

Then add them all up:
6 + 14 + 14 + 48 + 30 + 30 + 16π = **(142 + 16π) cm²**

For the perimeter take each part in turn again.

Head 1) c = 2πr = 2π × 4 = 8π.
(2cm is hidden by the neck)   so c = **8π – 2cm**
Neck 2) Only 2 sides are not hidden so the perimeter is 3 + 3 = **6cm**
Left arm 3) 2 sides + 1 end are not hidden so 7 + 7 + 2 = **16cm**
Right arm 4) 2 sides + 1 end are not hidden so 7 + 7 + 2 = **16cm**
Body 5) Top 6cm – 2cm hidden = 4cm, sides 2 (8cm – 2cm hidden)
= 12cm + lower edge 6cm – 2 × 2cm = **2cm,**
    Total 4 + 12 + 2 = **18cm**
Left leg 6) Sides 2 × 15cm + lower edge 2cm = **32cm**
Right Leg 7) Sides 2 × 15cm + lower edge 2cm = **32cm**

Then add up (8π - 2) + 6 + 16 + 16 + 18 + 32 + 32 = **(8π +120) cm**

So, the area = (142 + 16π) cm² = 237·1cm²
and the perimeter = (120 + 8π) cm = 145.1cm

This example has given you 7 areas and 7 perimeters to find.

Now do exercise 42.

Chapter 42 - Areas and Perimeters of Shapes

Exercise 42

Use the value of π which is given by your calculator or π = 3.14

1) In a lawn there are 3 circular flower beds edged with clay pavers. One is 7m in diameter; the other two are 4m in diameter. What is the area and circumference of all three beds?

2) A water feature consists of two circular ponds 5m in diameter connected by a channel 1m wide and 10m long. What is the area of the water and the total circumference of the feature.

3) A rectangular blue carpet covers a floor measuring 10m by 6m. A rectangular hole measuring 8m by 4m was cut out of the blue carpet and the hole filled with gold carpet. Find
    a) the area of the blue carpet,
    b) the area of the gold carpet, and
    c) the distance round the edges of both carpets

4) A corridor 20m long is tilled in a zig-zag pattern with black

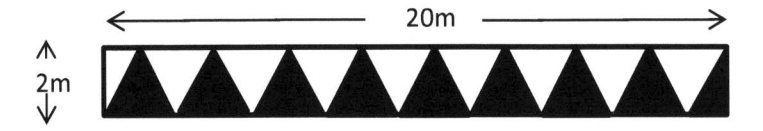

and white tiles. What is the area of each coloured area?

5) A pattern of seven tiles, each with sides 0·5 m long is built into a wall. What is the area of the pattern and what is its outside perimeter?

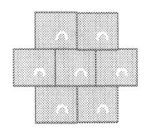

Key Stage 3 Maths Explained - Volume 2 Geometry

Answers to Exercise 42

1) The area of each 4m flower bed

is $\pi \times \left(\dfrac{diameter}{2}\right)^2 = \pi \times \left(\dfrac{4}{2}\right)^2 = 12\cdot57m^2$

the area of each 7m flower bed

is $\pi \times \left(\dfrac{diameter}{2}\right)^2 = \pi \times \left(\dfrac{7}{2}\right)^2 = 38\cdot48m^2$

So, the total area of the flower beds is

$2 \times 12\cdot57m^2 + 38\cdot48m^2 = 63\cdot62m^2$

2) The area of the 5m circular pond is

is $\pi \times \left(\dfrac{diameter}{2}\right)^2 = \pi \times \left(\dfrac{4}{2}\right)^2 = 12\cdot57m^2$

3)   a) $10 \times 6 = 60m^2$
         b) $8 \times 4 = 32m^2$
         c) Blue carpet $10 + 10 + 6 + 6 = 32m$,
            Gold carpet $8 + 8 + 4 + 4 = 24m$

4 The total area of the seven tiles is $7(0\cdot5 \times 0\cdot5) = 1\cdot75m^2$

The perimeter round the seven tiles is
$2 \times (0\cdot5 + 0\cdot5 + 0\cdot25 + 0\cdot5 + 0\cdot25 + 0\cdot5 + 0\cdot5) = 2 \times 6 = 12m$

Chapter 43 – Pentagons, Hexagons and Octagons

Pentagons, Hexagons and Octagons. These shapes all have Greek names. Penta refers to five, hexa to six, and octa to eight. (It's just that Greek mathematicians thought of them first.) The general name for geometric figures with many sides is **Polygon** (poly means many).

A triangle has **three sides** and the sizes of its three angles add up to **180°**.

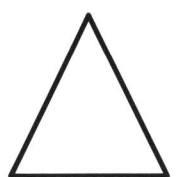

Add another side and you have a Rectangle or a quadrilateral with **four sides** whose angles add up to 180° + 180° = **360°**.

Add a further side and you get a **pentagon** (five sides and five angles) whose angles add up to (I hope you've guessed it), 360° + 180° = 540°.
In a regular pentagon, like the one Illustrated, each internal angle is 108°

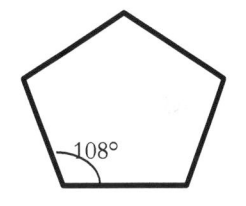

Add another side and you have a **hexagon,** with six sides whose six angles add up to
540° + 180° = 720°. In a regular hexagon each internal angled is 120°

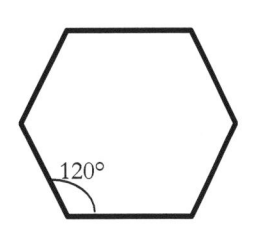

Key Stage 3 Maths Explained - Volume 2 Geometry

A seven-sided figure is called a **heptagon** with seven sides and seven angles. These add up to 720° + 180° = 900° A regular heptagon has internal angles of 108°.

Finally, an eight-sided figure is called an **Octagon.** Its internal angles add up to 1080° A regular octagon has internal angles of 135 °

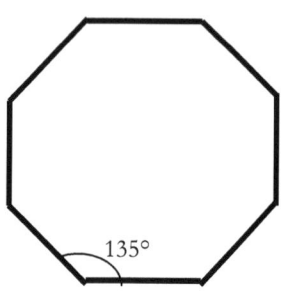

However much a polygon is distorted, Its internal angles will always add up to the number for that particular polygon.

The side lengths and angles of this rectangle are all different, but its internal angles still add up to 360°

All the sides of this triangle have been extended to create three **external angles**, marked $x°$, $y°$ and $z°$, $x° + y° + z° = 360°$

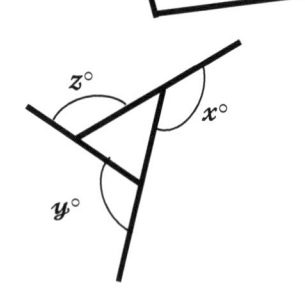

The external angles of all polygons
It doesn't matter what their shape or however many sides they have, will always add up to 360°. This makes sense because the more sides you add the nearer the polygon gets to being a circle and the angled right round a circle is 360°.

As an exercise on this chapter, please memorize the new names pentagon, hexagon, heptagon and octagon, and the sizes of the internal and external angles of each.

Chapter 44 – Volumes of Cubes and Cuboids

Volume of a Cuboid

Look at this cube.
It takes up space.
The space it takes up is its volume.

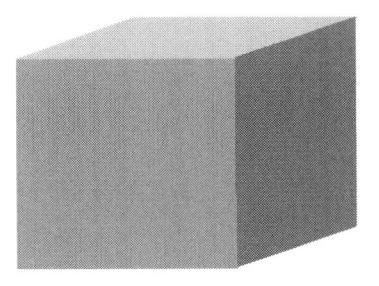

This cube is just a drawing, so look
at a box of tissues or
breakfast cereal.

How do we measure volume?

We started by measuring length in meters or centimeters. Then we measured area in square centimeters. Now we are going to use a cube with sides of one centimeter to measure volume. A cube with sides of one centimeter has a volume of one cubic centimeter.

To measure a cereal box, we must measure its length, its width and its height.

The length × the width
= the area of **the base of the box**
This tells you how many 1cm squares there are in the base.

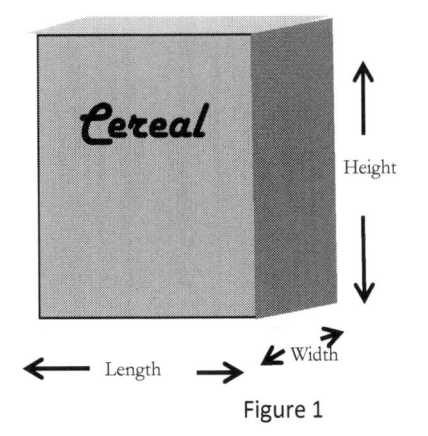

Figure 1

Key Stage 3 Maths Explained - Volume 2 Geometry

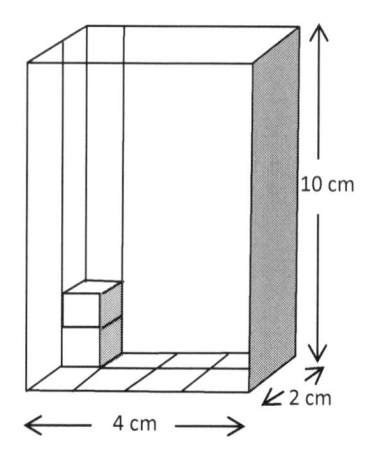

Figure 2

On each square centimeter of the base you could stand a 1-centimeter cube and build a column of cubes (1cm × 1cm × 10cm) one for each centimeter of the height. (Figure 2)

If the width is 4cm, and the depth 2cm then the area of the base would be 2 × 4 = 8 square cm.
If the height is 10cm you could get 10 cubes in a column on each square
(I show only the first 2 here).

So, the **volume of the box** is 2 × 4 × 10 = 80 cubic centimeters

We could put a column of ten cubes on each of the eight squares on the bottom. Eight columns of cubes can be fitted into the box. So, the number of cubes which will fit into the box is the number of cubes in each column, which is ten, times the number of columns, which is 2 × 4 = 8. As 10 × 8 = 80 this shows that the volume of the box (or cuboid) is found by multiplying the length by the width by the height.

Chapter 44 – Volumes of Cubes and Cuboids

To find the volume of any rectangular box, we multiply its width by its depth to get the area of its base, and then multiply this area by the height of the box to find the volume. The volume of the box is its width × its depth × height. Each of these three lengths is measured in centimeters so we multiplied cm × cm × cm. When three of the same things are multiplied together we can write this as cm^3 with a small 3 at the top. We read this as centimeters cubed and say that the volume of the box is 2 × 4 × 10 = 80 cm^3.

Figure 3 shows another box. (Its proper name is cuboid.) It is 15 cm long, 10 cm wide and 5 cm high. Its volume is its length times its width times its height. That is 15 cm for its length times 10 cm for its width, times 5 cm for its height. Multiplying 15 × 10 × 5 = 750, and multiplying cm × cm × cm is cm cubed, so the volume of this cuboid is 750 cm^3.

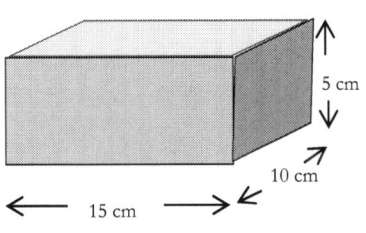

Figure 3

Exercise 44

1. A cereal packet is 19cm wide, 8cm deep and 30cm high. What is its volume?

2. Find the volume of a paper handkerchief box which measures 16cm by 31cm by 5cm.

3. Find the volume of a cube which measures 2·5m × 2·5m × 2·5m.

4. A swimming pool measures 100m by 15m and is 2m deep. What is its volume?

5. A flat roofed house is 10·5m wide, 7·3m deep and 6m high. What is its internal volume?

Key Stage 3 Maths Explained - Volume 2 Geometry

Answers to Exercise 44

1) The volume of the cereal packet is 4560cm³

2) The volume of the handkerchief box is 2480cm³

3) The volume of the 2·5m cube is 15·625m³

4) The volume of the swimming pool is 3000m³

5) The volume of the house is 5499m³

A tip from your Tutor

In questions like this always say what you are calculating:
"The volume of the handkerchief box is"
and give the units after your answer. **"cm³"**

Chapter 45 - Prisms Pyramids and Cylinders

Prisms have parallel edges.
Cuboids which we studied in the last chapter could also be called prisms.

Figure 1 is a cuboid, the shape of a brick. Its longer edges are parallel. Its two ends are exactly the same shape. It is a prism

These edges are parallel

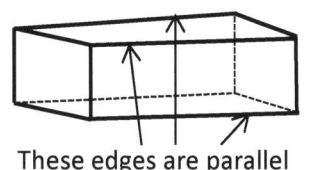

Figure 1

If you made the cuboid of modeling clay you could cut it in two. If you cut it parallel to either end, the new 'ends' would look exactly like one of the original ones. (Figure 2)

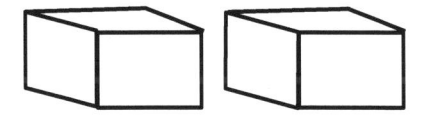

Figure 2

Another prism might have triangular ends, like the one in figure 3,

but the edges are still parallel, and both ends are the same size and shape.

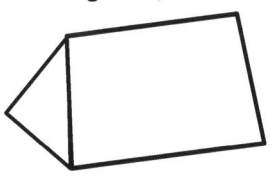

Figure 3

Again, if you cut a triangular prism it in two, (figure 4) You would end up with two more ends like the original ones.

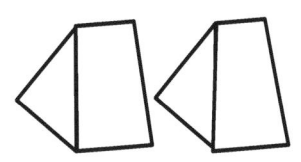

Figure 4

193

Key Stage 3 Maths Explained - Volume 2 Geometry

A cylinder (figure 5) such as a stick of rock is also **a prism**, or at least that is what it is called in geometry. It doesn't have any edges along its length, but like the other two prisms you could cut it anywhere along its length and make a new end which would be exactly the same shape and area as the original end.

Figure 5

You could have star shaped prisms, or prisms with any regular or irregular shape, so long as its cross section does not change anywhere along its length. You must be able to cut it in two, anywhere along its length, and make two new ends which are the same size and shape as its original ends.

Volume of a prism

How do we calculate the volume of a prism? Provided that the ends are at right angles to its length, this is very simple. Multiply the area of one end by the length to get the volume.

The volume of the rectangular prism of figure 6 is the area of an end multiplied by the length

Volume = height × breadth × length

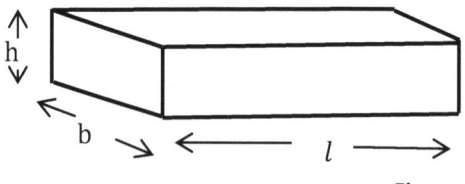

Figure 6

The surface area of this prism is the surface area of all its six faces. That is the area of the two ends which is 2(h × b) plus the area of the two sides 2(l × h), plus the area of the top and bottom 2(b × l)

So, the total surface area A = 2(h × b) + 2(l × h) + 2(b × l)

Chapter 45 - Prisms Pyramids and Cylinders

For example, if you are asked to find the surface area and volume of a rectangular prism 10cm long, 3cm high and 4cm wide, you would calculate the surface area as:

Multiply the numbers in the brackets then add

A = 2(3 × 4) + 2(10 × 3) + 2(4 × 10)
= 24 + 60 + 80 = 164cm²

The volume of this prism is height × breadth × length

Don't forget the units cm³

= 3 × 4 × 10cm³
= 120cm³

Now for the triangular prism, (Figure 7)

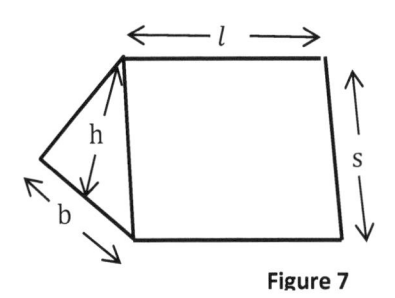

Its volume is calculated as the area of the triangular ends times the length (The area of the ends is ½ base × the height.)

Figure 7

So, the volume of the triangular prism = ½ b × h × l
The surface area of a triangular prism is surface area is the area of the two triangular ends, (each ½ b × h)
plus the areas of its three rectangular sides,
(two sloping sides and the base)
The area of the base is b × l.
The area of each sloping side is s × l,

So, the total area is 2 × (½b × h) + (b × l) + 2(s × l)

Key Stage 3 Maths Explained - Volume 2 Geometry

For the circular prism in figure 8 the volume would be the area of an end which is πr^2, where r is the radius of the circular end, times l which is the length of the prism. The volume of a cylinder (or circular prism) = $\pi r^2 l$

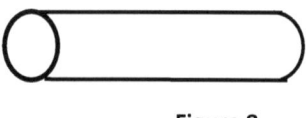

Figure 8

To find Its surface area imagine wrapping a piece of paper round the cylinder and then trimming the paper until it just fitted

When you un-wrapped it you would have a piece of paper whose length was the length l of the cylinder and whose width was
$2 \times \pi \times r$
where r is the radius of the cylinder.
Then you have to add the area of the two ends each of which is $\pi \times r^2$.

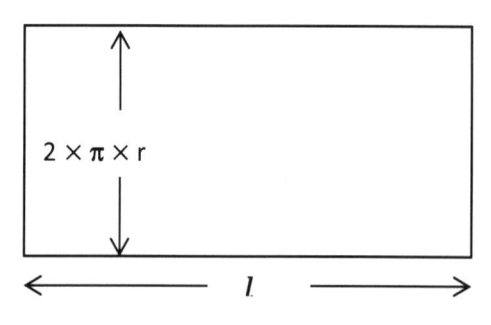

Figure 9

So, the surface area of a cylinder is $2 \times \pi \times r \times l + 2 (\pi \times r^2)$

If you had a stick of rock 5cm in diameter and 30cm long its volume would be
V = $\pi r^2 l$ = $\pi \times 2\cdot 5^2 \times 30$ cm³

   = $\pi \times 6\cdot 25 \times 30$ cm³

   = $187\cdot 5 \pi$

   = 589cm³

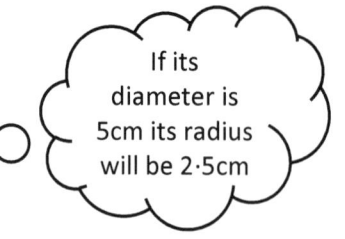

If its diameter is 5cm its radius will be 2·5cm

Its surface area would be
Area = $2 \times \pi \times r \times l + 2 (\pi \times r^2)$
     = $2 \times \pi \times 2\cdot 5 \times 30 + 2 (\pi \times 2\cdot 5^2)$cm²
     = $15\cdot 71 + 39\cdot 27 = 54\cdot 98$cm²

Chapter 45 - Prisms Pyramids and Cylinders

Exercise 45

(give your answers to 3 significant figures, π = 3.14

1) A rectangular prism has a height of 10cm, a length of 20cm and a width of 15cm. What is its volume?

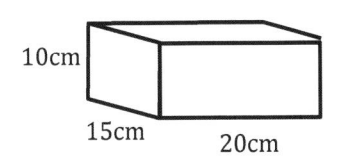

2) 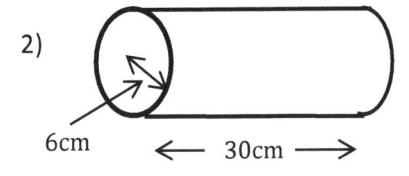 A cylinder is 30cm long has a radius of 6cm. What is its volume? What is its outside area?

3) A triangular prism has a base 10cm wide, a height of 12cm and is 20cm long.
a) What is its volume?
b) What is it outside area? 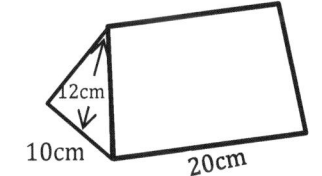
(Hint: use the Pythagoras formula to find the length of the sloping sides)

4) Another cylinder is 25cm long has a radius of 15cm. What is its volume? What is its outside area?

5) A shed is 5m long, 3m wide and has walls 2.5m high. The roof is 1m higher than the top of the wall. What is its volume?

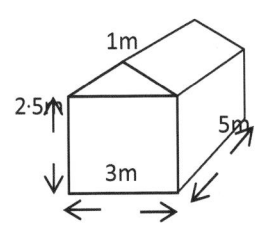

Key Stage 3 Maths Explained - Volume 2 Geometry

Answers to Exercise 45

1) The volume is: $10 \times 15 \times 30 = 3000 \text{cm}^3$

2) The volume of the cylinder is:
$30 \times \pi \times 6^2 = 3391 \text{cm}^3$

2 ends

Its surface area is $2 \times \pi \times 6^2$ for the ends
plus $2 \times \pi \times 6 \times 30$ for the cylinder = $226 + 1130 = 1356 \text{cm}^2$

3) The volume is the area of one end multiplied by the length
That is $½ \times 12 \times 10 \times 20 = 1200 \text{cm}^3$

Its surface area is the area of both ends
plus the areas of the three rectangular sides.
The length of the sloping sides is
$\sqrt{5^2 + 12^2} = \sqrt{25 + 144} = \sqrt{169} = 13 \text{cm}$

Remember, multiply before you add

The surface area is:
$2 \times ½ \times 12 \times 10 + 2 \times 13 \times 20 + 10 \times 20 \text{cm}^3$
$= 120 + 520 + 200 = 840 \text{cm}^3$

4) The volume of the cylinder is: $25 \times \pi \times 15^2 = 17662 \text{cm}^3$
Its surface area is $2 \times \pi \times 15^2$ for the ends
plus $2 \times \pi \times 6 \times 30$ for the cylinder = $226 + 565 = 791$

5) First look at the lower part. This is a rectangular block
$2·5 \times 3 \times 5 = 37·5 \text{m}^3$.
The roof is a triangular prism with a volume of
$½ \times 3 \times 5 = 7·5 \text{m}^3$

So, the total volume of the shed is $37·5 + 7·5 = 44·5 \text{m}^3$

Chapter 46 – Regular Solids

There are just five regular solids. Each of these has a number of identical flat faces. If you turn them round each face looks just the same.

The simplest of these is a triangular pyramid made up of four isosceles triangles, (Figure 1). It has four identical faces and is known as a **tetrahedron**. (tetra is the Greek for four)

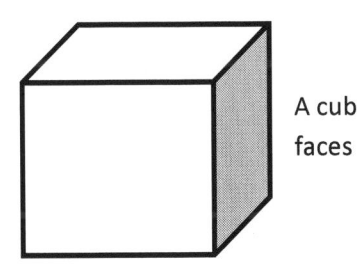

Figure 1

A cube, figure 2, has six identical square faces

Figure 2

An **Octahedron** has eight identical faces each of which is an isosceles triangle. This is illustrated in figure 3

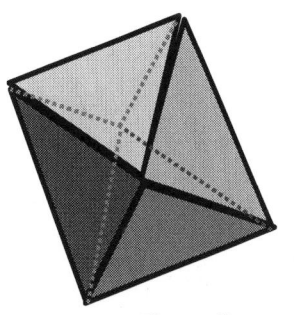

Figure 3

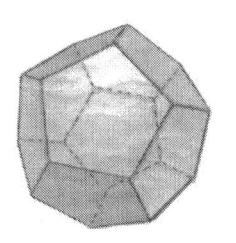

(Octo means eight, an octopus has eight legs)

A **Dodecahedron** (figure 4) has twelve identical faces in the form of regular pentagrams. Each pentagram has five sides.

Key Stage 3 Maths Explained - Volume 2 Geometry

The fifth and last of these regular solids is the **Icosahedron**, made up of twenty identical isosceles triangles. It is illustrated in figure 5

Figure 5

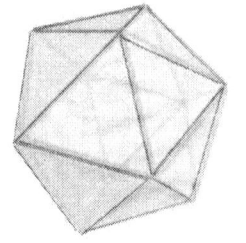

These regular solids were known to the Greek philosophers and described in a book written by the Greek philosopher Plato who lived from about 427 BC to – 348 BC.
For this reason, they are sometimes known as Platonic Solids.

You can find a proof that only five such solids can exist, in Wikipedia, No other regular solids can exist in three-dimensional space. The earliest form of this proof was given by Euclid, another Greek Philosopher.

There is one surprising fact about all solids made up of <u>plane surfaces</u>:

It doesn't work with curved surfaces

The number of surfaces (**S**)+number of corners (**C**) – number of edges (**E**) = 2

Here are some examples:

	Surfaces	Corners	Edges	S + C – E
Cuboid	6	8	12	2
Triangular Prism	5	6	9	2
Hexagonal Prism	8	12	18	2
Triangular base pyramid	4	4	6	2
Square based pyramid	5	5	8	2

This is true of all solids made up of plane surfaces, not just regular solids.

As an exercise on this chapter, memorize **S + C – E = 2**

Chapter 47 – Spheres and Cones

Spheres come in all sizes, but all have the same basic shape
The Earth is almost spherical, if we ignore the roughness's on its surface caused by mountains and the depths under the seas. Strictly however it is not quite spherical because the force caused by its spinning on its axis has caused it to bulge a little at the equator and shrink a little at the poles.
This shape is called an **Oblate Spheroid**

The two main things about a sphere is its surface area and its volume.

Remember

The surface area of a sphere is given by: s = $4\pi r^2$,
where r is the radius of the sphere.
How do you measure the radius of a sphere?
The practical way of finding the diameter of a small sphere is to have a metal plate with a row of holes drilled in it of increasing sizes. Find the smallest hole that the sphere will fall through, and measure the diameter of the hole. The radius is the half the diameter.

Remember

The volume of a sphere is given by the formula $v = \frac{4}{3}\pi r^3$

These formulae can be found by imagining a sphere cut into a large number of thin slices. Figure 1 shows a sphere cut up in this way.

The surface area is found by finding the area round the edge of each slice, and the volume of the sphere found by adding up the volumes of all the disks. As you cut it into more and more slices, the slope on the edge of each slice becomes

Figure 1

less and less important, and your answer gets more accurate. To do this correctly you will need to understand Integration, which you come to later. So, for now, just accept and use the formulae.

Key Stage 3 Maths Explained - Volume 2 Geometry

The cone illustrated in figure 2 is described as a **right circular cone**. Its base is a circle, radius r, and its apex (the point at the top) is directly Above the center of its circular base, which is why it is described as "right".

The **volume of a right circular cone** Is $\frac{1}{3} \pi r^2 h$. (and you need to add the units in which the height and radius are measured) such as cm, So, the volume is then in cm³.

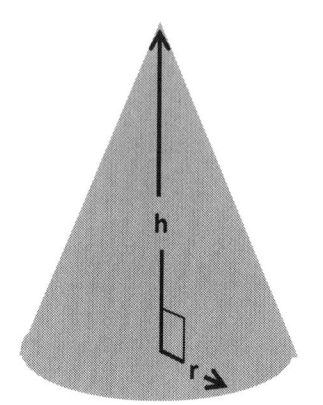

As with the sphere, the formula can be found by dividing the cone into a series of slices (figure 3). By making the number of slices larger and larger and each slice thinner and thinner, you get a progressively better approximation to the volume of a cone.

Figure 3

To find the surface area of a cone imagine rapping a piece of paper round its surface and cutting it to fit. When laid out flat, the paper would look like a slice out of a circle (Figure 4). The radius of the circle would be the distance down the side of the cone which would be $\sqrt{h^2 + r^2}$ (using the Pythagoras formula)

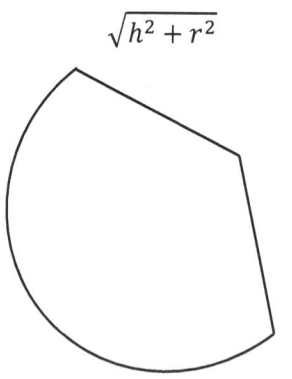

Figure 4

202

Chapter 47 – Spheres and Cones

and the distance round the base of the cone, which is $2\pi r$ is the length around the slice.
(In geometry the slice is called **the segment of the circle**)

The area of the whole circle is just $\pi(\sqrt{h^2+r^2})^2 = \pi(h^2 + r^2)$
The circumference of the whole circle is $2\pi\sqrt{h^2+r^2}$

The segment is however only $\dfrac{2\pi r}{2\pi\sqrt{h^2+r^2}}$ of the whole circle

So, the area of the segment is $\dfrac{\cancel{2\pi}\, r}{\cancel{2\pi}\sqrt{h^2+r^2}} \times \pi(h^2 + r^2)$

Which is **the surface area of a cone** = $\pi r \sqrt{h^2 + r^2}$

Exercise 47

1) A beach ball has a diameter of 0·8m. What is its volume?

2) A balloon is blown up with helium until its diameter is 30cm.
   a) If a liter of helium is 1000cm³, how many liters will this take?
   b) what is the surface area of the balloon?

3) The circumference of the Earth is about 40000 kilometers.
   If the Earth was a perfect sphere,
   a) What would its volume be in km³?
   b) What is its surface area in km²?

4) A monument made like a right circular cone is to be built.
It is to be 50m tall and with a radius at its base of 5m
a) What is the area of its conical surface?
b) What is its volume?

5) A blunt cone is 15cm high and
measures 10cm across the base (its diameter).
a) Find its volume
b) Find the area of its sloping side
c) Find the area of its base

Key Stage 3 Maths Explained - Volume 2 Geometry

Answers to exercise 47

1) The beach ball has a diameter of 0·8m so its radius is 0·4m

Its volume is $V = \frac{4}{3}\pi r^3 = \frac{4}{3}\pi \times 0.4^3 = 0.268$ m³

2) The diameter of the balloon is 30cm so its radius as 15cm.

a) Its volume in liters is $= \frac{4}{3}\pi \times 15^3 \div 1000 = 14.13$ liters

b) The surface area of the balloon is $S = 4\pi r^2 = 11304$ cm²

3) The circumference of the Earth is about 40,000 km,

So, its radius, r is: $\frac{40000}{2\pi} = 6369$ km, and

a) its volume is $= \frac{4}{3}\pi r^3 = \frac{4}{3}\pi\, 258353141409$ km³

$= 1081,638,485,365$ km³

b) the surface area of the earth is $4\pi r^2 = 509,485,862$ km²

4 a) The surface area $= \pi r\sqrt{h^2 + r^2} = \pi r\sqrt{50^2 + 5^2}$

$= \pi \times 5 \times \sqrt{(2500 + 25)} = 789$m²

The volume of the cone is $= \frac{1}{3}\pi r^2 h = \frac{1}{3} \times \pi \times 5^2 \times 50 = 1308$m³

5) a) The volume of the cone $= \frac{1}{3}\pi \times 5^2 \times 15 = 392$cm³

b) The sloping surface area is $= \pi r\sqrt{15^2 + 5^2}$
$= \pi \times 5 \times 15.81 = 248$cm²

c) The area of its base $= \pi \times r^2 = 3.14 \times 5^2 = 78.5$cm²

Chapter 48 – Things to Remember

You will find it helps if you memorize the following names and rules and advice.

The reciprocal of a number is 1 divided by the number.
The **reciprocal** of 5 is $\frac{1}{5}$. The reciprocal of x is $\frac{1}{x}$. (page 19)

Do keep the **calculation**s, like (16 × 4 and 69 ÷ 3) beside your working (Page 24).

Powers outside a Bracket $3(xy)^3 a$. The power, the little 3, applies to both the x and the y which are inside the bracket, but not to anything outside. Not to the 3 or the **a**. (page 20)

Remember, **multiply before you add** (Page 23)

Graphs with **negative slopes;** you just have to remember that as x gets bigger y gets smaller.
The lines slope down from left to right. (page 42)

For any **arithmetic series** you need:
    the number you start with,
    The standard difference
    The number of terms you need. (Page 51)

In any series **the number you started with is the first number.**
So, if you want six terms you add another five terms (Page 61)

An equation is like a seesaw. You must always do the same thing to **both side of the equation**. (or it won't balance). (Page 67)

Four rules for **rearranging equations.** (Pages 68 and 69)

A Coefficient is a fixed number like **a** or 5 which multiplies a variable number like x or y (Page 81)

Key Stage 3 Maths Explained - Volume 2 Geometry

For any number n, **n² = -n × -n as well as n × n**. (Page 91)

Learn how to **bisect a line,** (Page 136 -137)
Construct a right angle,
and bisect an angle (page 138 – 140)

There are five types of triangle: (Page 142)
Scalene triangles, (any shape)
Isosceles triangles, (two equal angles and two identical sides)
Equilateral triangles, (three angles of 60° and three equal sides)
Right angled triangles (one angle is 90°)
Obtuse angle triangles. (one angle is more than 90°)

Acute Angles are angles which are less than 90° (Page 143)

The three **angles inside all triangles add up to 180°**. (Page 143)

Congruent triangles have the same angles and are the same size.
Similar Triangles have the same angles but may be of different sizes. (page 150)
To work out a **perimeter.** Add the lengths of all the outside sides (remember the perimeter ant). (Page 165)

The Pythagoras formula only works with **right angle triangles** on a **plane** (that is a flat) surface (Page 175)

The circumference of a circle radius **r** is $c = 2\pi r$ (Page 178)
The area A of a circle of radius **r** is $A = \pi r^2$ (Page 178)

The volume of a cylinder is, length l, radius r is $\pi r^2 l$ (Page 196)
The surface area of a cylinder is $2\pi r l + 2(\pi \times r^2)$ (Page 201)

The surface area of a sphere is given by: $s = 4\pi r^2$ (Page 201)
The volume of a sphere is $v = \frac{4}{3}\pi r^3$ (page 197)

Chapter 48 - How to Pass Examinations

Exams!

There are several things I tell all my pupils about passing examinations.

A final tip from your tutor

1. Work out a revision plan well ahead of the actual examination. Don't leave it until the last few days before the examination, or worse, until the evening before!

2. Look at past papers and work out how much time you can afford to spend on each question.

3. If you can, give yourself a day off from the subject of tomorrow's exam. Get a good night's sleep so that you arrive refreshed and rested.

4. Outside the examination room, don't stand with a group of friends asking "have you revised……?" It will only remind you of the things you have forgotten to revise.

5. Bring a favorite book to read while you wait to go into the examination. It stops you thinking, or talking to friends, about the things you have **not** revised! Your invigilator will take care of the book for you. **Don't** forget to hand it over as you go in or you could be in trouble! (And ask for it back when the examination is over)

6. When the exam starts, put your pen **down**. Read the paper and pick the easiest question. Do that one first; it will give you confidence. Then choose the best of the rest. That way you leave the worst question until last. It is the one which will give you fewest marks.

7. Write down the number of minutes you have. Divide that by the total number of marks available for the whole exam. Time yourself for the number of minutes per mark. That will tell you how long you should spend on each question.

8. When you have picked a question; **read it carefully.** You can't give a good answer if you have only just glanced at it. Don't spend too long on a difficult question. It may stop you answering an easier one.

9. Explain your workings and keep your answers neat. Examiners have only a little time to look at each answer. If they can't quickly understand what you are doing, you will lose marks. If the answer is a number or a mathematical expression. For example, if you have been asked to find the value of y, write "$y = 2x + 3$" and PUT IN THE UNITS, if there are any: Don't leave the examiner to guess which of several bits of maths you meant as the answer!

10. Keep an eye on the clock. Don't spend too long on a difficult question. It may stop you answering an easier one. Leaving a question incomplete won't cost you many marks. (I know, I have been an examiner.)

11. **Don't Panic!**
In an examination, if you start to feel a little bit anxious, worried or even a bit panicky, this is what you should do.
Put down your pen
Close your eyes
Picture somewhere nice, somewhere you have felt calm and happy. You could think of a garden, the seaside, a lake, a wood, or a country valley; anywhere which feels right to you. Breathe in counting slowly to five. Breathe out again slowly. Do this three times. It will only take about thirty seconds. Open your eyes and look at the problem again

12. If possible finish about five or ten minutes early so that you have time to read through your answers and correct any minor slips.

13. I wish you every possible success in your examinations. Good Luck!

Index

	Chapter	Page
Acute	34	143
Adjacent	34	143
Angles (definition and notation)	31	129
(Measurement)	31	130
Area (Circle)	41	177
(Rectangle)	37	159
(Triangle)	39	167
Arithmetic Series	13	45
Base (base number, of a logarithm)	29	124
(Base of a triangle)	38	163
(Base of a cuboid)	43	189
Base Line (mapping)	35	152
Bisecting		
Angles	33	138
Lines or distances	33	137
Brackets	5	19
Multiplying	24	105
Center of a circle (definition)	41	177
(Finding the center of a circle)	41	181
Changing the subject of an equation	19	71
Circumference	41	177
Coefficient	22	81
Common Difference	14	47
Congruent Triangles	35	150
Cones	47	202
Cube Roots	4	15
Cubes	4	15
Cuboids	44	189
Cylinders	45	194
Drawing and Measuring Lines and Angles	31	129
Diameter	41	177
Equations (definition)	1	3
(rearranging)	19	67, 68
(Word equations)	2	7
External Angles of a Triangle	34	146
of a Polygon	43	188
Exponential	29	123
(**e** the exponential)	29	125
Expressions	19	70
Factors, What are they?	24	101
Multiplying Factors	25	103
Multiplying Brackets	26	105
Fibonacci Series	18	63
Geometric Series	17	59
Hexagons	43	187

209

Key Stage 3 Maths Explained - Volume 2 Geometry

gHyperbola			30	127
Hypotenuse			37	143
Inequalities	(See Part1 Chapter 39 page 192)			
Indices	(Chapter 3 pages 11, 12, and 13)	and	29	123
Isosceles Triangles			34	142
Linear Equations			6	23
Linear Equations	(graphs)		10	37
Measuring	(Angles)		31	130
	(lines)		32	133
Normal			33	136
Obtuse Angles			34	143
Opposite Angles			34	143
Perimeters of:	Circles		41	177
	Parallelograms		39	168
	Rectangles		39	167
Parallel Lines	(light from a star)		23	91
	(Definition)		33	135
	(Prisms)		45	193
Perpendicular Lines			33	136
Pentagons			43	187
Pi (π)			41	177
Powers			3	11 to 12
Power curve			29	124
Polygons			43	187
Prisms			45	191
Protractor			31	130
Pythagoras			40	173
Quadrants			12	44
Quadratic Equations	23	86 and	28	113
Radius			41	177
Reciprocals			5	19
Rearranging Equations			19	67 to 71
Rectangle	36	155, 156 and	39	167
Right angles			33	136
Right angled Triangles			40	173
Roots	(square roots, cube roots and n^{th} roots)		4	15
	(roots of an equation)		23	89
Similar Triangles			35	149, 150
Spheres			47	201
Square Roots			4	15
Terms	(in a series)		13	46
	(in an equation)		19	67
Volumes of	Cubes and cuboids		44	190
	Cones		47	202
	Prisms		45	194
	Spheres		47	201

210

Printed in Great Britain
by Amazon